12.21.79

Fixing Furniture

Peter Jones

Butterick Publishing

Design by Remo Cosentino
Illustrations by Gary Tong

Library of Congress Cataloging in Publication Data

Jones, Peter, 1934–
   Fixing furniture.

   Includes index.
   1. Furniture—Repairing. I. Title.
TT199.J66   684.1   79–13915
ISBN 0–88421–067–7

CONTENTS

THE BASICS
OF FURNITURE REPAIR

Unlike most of the products you purchase today, furniture, even inexpensive furniture, is made to last. It is not constructed with a built-in obsolescence that will make it crumble three months after you have paid off the two-year loan you took out to buy it in the first place. And if it is a quality piece to begin with, you can expect it to go on withstanding normal use for at least your lifetime, and probably the lifetime of your grandchildren.

The reason furniture remains so durable is because of the materials used to make it and the ways in which it is constructed. The basic material used in furniture is wood, and no matter what our society does to its economy, nature keeps on making wood in the same old way—to last. Nature hasn't learned any cheaper production methods that will turn out more trees faster at the expense of the strength or beauty of the wood.

The other reason furniture remains such a high-quality product is that there are only a few proven ways of putting wood together in the form of a chair, a table or a piece of casework, and these assembly techniques and procedures simply cannot be fudged. The wood has to go together in one of only a few ways or the legs will wobble, the table will sag in the middle or the casework will be rickety.

Daily use, changes in the weather and the passage of time all conspire to disintegrate any piece of furniture. Joints between various parts of a piece can work loose under the pressure of repeated battering and stress. Or the joints may loosen simply because humid weather has caused the wood to swell, then shrink back to its normal size as the cold air of winter settles around it. Furniture parts, particularly the legs and arms of chairs, can crack or break. The finish, once applied in a long, careful process, can become stained or scratched or marred. After years of being bombarded by liquids and dirt, wax, sharp objects and the weather, it may eventually reach the point where it can no longer be repaired, but must be entirely removed and replaced.

Still, with a modest amount of time and effort in cleaning, polishing, regluing, removing scratches and raising dents, you can extend the life of any piece of furniture almost indefinitely. It can be rejuvenated because one of the blessings of wood is that it can almost always be returned to its original state. Scratches can be filled, dents raised or filled, rough surfaces evened and sanded smooth again; the joints can be reglued or strengthened; all of the parts can be disassembled, then put back together once again. To do all that to a discarded piece of "junk" can be very rewarding, for after long hours of labor will come a piece that is once again functional and decorative; add to this your personal satisfaction at devoting your time, money and effort to re-create something that is truly useful and attractive.

Doing Your Own Restoration

There is nothing difficult about restoring furniture. You need no particular talent, and none of the skills involved are so complicated that the average person cannot master them. You do not need many special tools either, but you do have to have a willingness to work long and hard. And it helps if you have a full appreciation and affection for wood and the other materials you are working with, as well as for the craftsmanship and talent that originally produced the furniture.

The furniture repairer has the singular aim of restoring part of another person's work. His objective is not to redesign or reconstruct the furniture, but to make it look more or less as it did when the original craftsman first completed it. Thus, when you set about the task of restoring furniture, you are attempting to duplicate someone else's craftsmanship successfully enough that the work you do cannot be detected by the casual observer. To accomplish this, you must have a lot of patience and use an abundance of loving care. With both of these, you can expect to develop a sense of which repair technique will work best in each situation you encounter. Assume that you will have to work and rework, and start over again from time to time. You will have to try different approaches and techniques, and learn from your errors. Whenever you approach a piece of furniture to be restored, you are in for a long, messy, seemingly thankless task that is rewarding only when you gaze at the finished work of art on a long winter's night and recall how miserable it looked before you started your restoration. Unless you take before and after pictures to show your friends, only you will ever know how much you have accomplished.

Tools of the Trade

Furniture is expensive. So is your time. If you plan to work with both commodities, don't jeopardize them by using inferior tools. That doesn't mean you should go out and blow your savings account on a lot of high-priced hardware, but it cautions you to decide which tools you need and then buy the best possible at the best bargain price you can find. It means skip the cheap imported screwdrivers and hammers you find as come-ons in supermarkets, but also be willing to put out enough money to buy a good electric drill and a vibrating sander if they are necessary to do a good job.

Nor do you have to buy a whole tool chest before you start work. Take your projects one at a time, and select the tools needed to finish only that project. As you take on more and more projects, you will gradually build up a complete cache of tools that can meet all of your needs.

The tools needed for restoring furniture divide into three categories: essential, optional and special.

ESSENTIAL TOOLS AND MATERIALS

No matter what furniture you are restoring, you will always need the following tools when repairing the structure or working on the finish.

Repair Work

Quarter-inch electric drill. Also buy a complete selection of high-speed bits, a sanding/buffing disk and a paint-stripper wheel.

Clamps. They come in all sizes and shapes. Ideally, you will eventually own at least one pair of each: C-clamps, adjustable hand screws, springs, pipe-bars, hold-downs, edge clamps, miters, bands and webs. Buy them as you need them; they each have specific purposes as well as ways of being used that will occur to you when you are trying to figure out how to hold two pieces of odd-shaped wood together. If you can buy only two clamps, the most versatile are the adjustable hand screws and the pipe-bar clamps, with the C-clamps running a close third.

Rope. You will need rope for tying tourniquets around the legs, arms and any other places your clamps are unable to get a good grip. Nylon is best, but clothesline will do.

Knives. You will find dozens of uses for a good, very sharp jackknife. Also have an old, dull kitchen knife for scraping off glue, cleaning out dowel holes and other assorted chores.

Mallet. This can be wooden, rubber or plastic, and is used for driving pieces of furniture together, as well as prying them apart, without damaging the wood.

Backsaw. This has a reinforcing rib along its back and is sold in several sizes; one with between 12 and 20 teeth per inch can handle most of the cutting chores you will face. The teeth are finer than those in either crosscut or rip saws, giving you a smoother cut in the wood. Backsaws are also used with miter boxes for cutting angled joints.

Plane. There are block planes, jack planes and the extremely long joiner planes. All of them will smooth and even wood, particularly along its edges. However, since furniture tends to have numerous small pieces, the block plane, which fits into your hand, is the most versatile tool to start with.

File, rasp and surform. These are all used to even off pieces of wood. Files and rasps may be round, triangular, square, rectangular and half round, and all come in a full range of coarsenesses. Surform tools are recent additions to your local hardware store's inventory and are essentially files with a handle. The cutting blade looks like a cheese grater and is extremely sharp. Surforms are easy to handle and excel when used on the edges of plywood because they cause a minimum of chipping in the face veneers. You will need an assortment of filing tools, but buy them as the need for them arises.

Sanding block. You can buy one or use a scrap chunk of 2″×4″ stock. Wrap sandpaper around the block and use it to achieve a more even sanding job, as well as reduce the damage to your hands.

Chisels. When you get into reshaping a joint or cleaning old glue off wood, a chisel can be indispensable; always keep it very sharp. To begin with acquire at least three, which have blade widths of ½″, ¾″ and 1″. You can buy any number of widths as you need them.

Nailset. This is good for knocking dowels out of their holes as well as driving nails below the surface of wood.

Hammer, screwdrivers, pliers, rules and combination squares. You probably already own all of these. If the furniture you are restoring contains a great many screws, consider purchasing a ratchet screwdriver, which has drill bits and both Phillips head and standard screwdriver blades. The ratchet driver will get screws in and out of wood a lot more quickly and easily than regular screwdrivers, with considerably less wear and tear on your hands.

Adhesives. There are dozens of adhesives on the market today, including modern (improved) versions of the traditional hide glues. The important facts to understand about glue used in furniture are that it must deliver tremendous pressure in pounds per square inch (psi), and it should be fairly rigid and usually water resistant. You cannot get all of these qualities in each of the modern fast-drying glues, which is why you need to own all those clamps. The following is a breakdown of glues recommended specifically for furniture manufacture and repair. All of them will work successfully if they are applied exactly according to the manufacturer's instructions.

■ *Acrylic* (3-Ton Adhesive glue). A mixture of a liquid and a powder that becomes rigid and delivers 6,000 psi. It will glue almost anything forever. Clamping time: 10 hours. Solvent: acetone (nail polish remover).

■ *Aliphatic* (Titebond glue). Sold as a one-part liquid. It is rigid and provides between 2,000 and 3,000 psi. Clamping time: 45 minutes, minimum. Solvent: warm water.

■ *Casein* (National Casein Co. #30 glue). Comes as a powder which you mix with water. It is rigid, delivers 3,200 psi and is especially good for such oily woods as lemon and teak. Clamping time: five to six hours. Solvent: warm water.

■ *Contact cement* (Weldwood Contact Cement). Used for bonding plastic laminates and wood veneers to core wood. It is a liquid that is painted on both gluing surfaces and allowed to dry for about 20 minutes. The coated surfaces will bond on contact. Clamping time: none. Solvent: acetone (nail polish remover).

■ *Hide glue* (Franklin Liquid Hide glue). Sold as a liquid or as flakes that are soaked in water. This is the traditional furniture glue; it offers 3,200 psi and is rigid. Clamping time: eight hours at 70°F. Solvent: warm water.

■ *Hot melt glue.* Comes in a 2″-long stick which is pushed through an electrically powered heat gun. It gives 250-plus psi and is flexible—good for filling gaps in loose joints. Clamping time: 60 seconds (don't clamp, just hold). Solvent: acetone (nail polish remover).

■ *Resorcinol* (Elmer's Waterproof glue). This has one part liquid and one part powder, and it can be used on boats as well as furniture. It is rigid, offers 3,400 psi and is very waterproof. Clamping time: four to 10 hours. Solvent: cool water (before it hardens).

■ *Urea formaldehyde* (Weldwood Plastic Resin glue). Comes as a powder to be mixed with water. It will give you 3,000 psi and is rigid. Clamping time: nine to 12 hours. Solvent: soap and water (before it hardens).

Abrasives. Abrasives used to be called sandpaper until the manufacturers stopped using sand to make them. Now flint, garnet, aluminum oxide or silicon carbide are used. Flint and garnet are natural materials, but are relatively softer than either aluminum oxide or silicon carbide, so they work best when you are hand-sanding. Aluminum oxide is the preferred abrasive for sanding hardwoods, which most of your good furniture is made of; silicon carbide is ideal for any of the softwoods as well as finish materials.

All abrasives can be purchased in a range of grits from very coarse to very fine. The very coarse and coarse grits are used for evening out rough, unfinished surfaces. The medium grits will remove any rough texture of the wood. Fine grits are used prior to applying a finish material. Only the very fine grits are used on the finish material itself.

Wood fillers. These include wood putty, dough and plastic wood. When they have hardened, all of them can be drilled, sawed or sanded. Which one you choose depends on your personal preference; experiment with different ones until you find the kind you like best.

Dowels. Most hardware stores sell 36″-long dowel sticks in varying diameters that can be cut to whatever lengths you need, usually about 1″. You can also buy packages of dowels already cut for you. Dowels are the major fastener used in most furniture, and if you need to use them extensively you will also require a set of doweling pins, if not a doweling jig (see page 15).

ABRASIVE SELECTION CHART

Grit	Grade	Description	Use
20	3	Very coarse	Machine floor-sanding. Never used on
24	3½	Very coarse	furniture.
30	2½	Coarse	Occasionally used for rough wood and
36	2	Coarse	paint removal.
40	1½	Coarse	
50	1	Medium	Preparatory wood sanding.
60	½	Medium	
80	1/0	Medium	
100	2/0	Fine	Softwood finish sanding.
120	3/0	Fine	Hardwood finish sanding.
150	4/0	Fine	
180	5/0	Fine	
220	6/0	Very Fine	Polishing finishes between coats.
240	7/0	Extra Fine	
280	8/0	Extra Fine	
320	—	Superfine	
360	9/0	Superfine	
400	10/0	Superfine	
500	—	Superfine	Rarely used on furniture. Primarily ap-
600	—	Superfine	plied to plastics, ceramics, stone and
			metals.

Silicon carbide or aluminum oxide is recommended for furniture work. Garnet is acceptable.

Screws, nails, angle irons and braces. You will very rarely use a common nail in any good furniture. Finishing nails show up occasionally. Screws are more common, but if a dowel and/or glue will hold the wood together, they are always preferable. As for using angle irons and braces, metal straps and so forth, the purists roll over in their graves at the idea. Even so, there are instances when screwing a piece of metal to a hidden part of the furniture will give added support to a joint, and is an excellent way of bracing.

Finish Work

Brushes old and new, and foam rubber paint pads. New brushes are used for applying finish materials. Old brushes are good for putting on paint removers, glues and other substances that will essentially end the usefulness of the brush. Better than any brush, the paint pads leave no bristle strokes and are disposable. Depending on the finish material you are applying, a paintbrush with either synthetic or natural bristles can be used. For most furniture work a brush width of 2″ should be sufficient. There may be times when you need an artist's brush for touchups and special effects. An old toothbrush that you have no intention of putting in your mouth again is good for scrubbing off paint and varnish that have been soaked in a chemical paint remover.

Tack rags. You can buy these at hardware or paint stores, or make them by sprinkling a solution of three parts turpentine and one part varnish on a clean, lint-free cloth that is about 1′ square. They are absolutely necessary for wiping off all the dust on any surface to be finished.

Putty knife and scrapers. A 1½″-wide putty knife has all kinds of uses, so it is good just to have around, and it is excellent for scraping away paint, glue and even wood fibers. A paint scraper is used to remove finish materials from large areas; you should buy one with a wide, replaceable blade.

Steel wool pads. Start by purchasing a package of assorted pads in grades from #1/0 to #3/0. You need steel wool to clean off messy residues left by paint and varnish removers, but the pads are also used during various stages of the finishing process.

Chemical paint removers. In general, the jellylike removers, which cling to a vertical surface, are best for all-around use. The brands on the market represent a wide range of paint-removing capabilities, and you will have to experiment with them until you find the one you like best.

Turpentine. This is used as a thinner with the polyurethanes and other varnishes, as well as for cleaning up yourself and your brushes.

Denatured alcohol. Alcohol has many thinning and cleaning uses, and is particularly helpful when you are dealing with shellac.

Linseed oil. Both raw and boiled linseed oil are useful to have around for restoring colors and even the wood itself. Keep a small can of each on hand.

Pumice and rottenstone. These are very fine powders used to hand-rub the final coat of any finish. There is no way you can get a perfect varnish or enamel topcoat without them.

Stains, fillers, bleaches, varnishes, shellacs and paint. The uses and descriptions of each of these finishing materials is discussed fully in Chapter 5.

OPTIONAL TOOLS AND MATERIALS

These are the tools and materials that are nice to have around, but should not be purchased until you have a specific need for them. You can do without most of them; it's just a whole lot easier to have them on hand.

Repair Work

Bit and brace. For many people, the old-fashioned hand-powered drill offers more control than an electric drill. In reality that is fallacious, but if you are comfortable with a hand-powered drill, there is no law against using it.

Center punch. This is handy for locating the exact center of wood that is to be drilled for dowels.

Doweling pins and jig. For less than $2, you can have a complete set of seven pins (or centers), each of a different diameter, each having a point extending from its exact center. You drill a hole for the dowel in one of the pieces to be joined, then insert whichever doweling pin fits in the hole and press the two pieces of wood together. The point on the pin will locate the center of the hole to be drilled in the opposite piece. The doweling jig is a more expensive, infinitely more accurate piece of equipment for locating dowel holes. It makes doweling a lark, but if you are doing anything less than making furniture, you probably don't need to go to the expense.

Drill press or drill stand. When you know where the dowel holes are positioned, you must then drill holes that will line up to form a straight channel through both pieces. A $400 drill press is perfect for drilling straight holes. A $20 drill stand that will hold your electric power drill in a vertical position is just as good.

Power sanders. You can buy a circular sanding disk for your electric drill for about $2. A vibrating sander costs around $15 and is well worth the money for finish sanding. For about $75 you can have a belt sander, which can do some marvelous smoothing very quickly; but merely restoring furniture may not warrant the cost.

Lathe. The only concerns that use lathes these days are furniture manufacturers, milling operations and people who get a kick out of turning wood. A lathe will, of course, reproduce a broken leg or chair spindle, but unless you are committed to the hobby of wood turning, skip the expense.

Radial arm saw. Even if you have never sawed a piece of wood before, the radial arm saw will make you an instant professional. Like the lathe, it needn't be bought unless you intend to do a lot of woodworking in addition to simply restoring furniture. If you do buy it, not only can you make crosscuts, rips, bevels, miters and compound saw cuts, but you can rout, dado, shape, sand, drill and even sharpen your other tools.

Bench saw. This tool is unparalleled for ripping lumber and, above all, extremely accurate for any cut you want to make. Again, if you are into a lot of carpentry, this is a tool you must have; it has only occasional application in the restoration of furniture.

Router. This neat little hand-held tool will shape edges and cut many joints, including the dovetails found in most fine furniture drawers. In fact, it is the only tool that will make dovetails effectively (provided you have a dovetail template to go with it) and trim the edges of plastic laminate neatly (provided you have a laminate trimmer accessory).

Saber saw. This is probably a good saw to have whether you are repairing furniture or doing any of a dozen other cutting chores around your home. It replaces the keyhole, compass and coping saws and will cut straight as well as curved lines and cutouts. Given the proper blade, a saber saw will work on any material from cardboard and leather to wood, plastic and metal, so it is well worth the $20 or so you have to pay for it.

Vise. Better than an extra pair of hands, a good vise will hold almost anything steady for you while you do whatever you want to do to the piece. Vises are normally bolted to the edge of a workbench.

Electric grinder. Any repair or restoration of furniture usually demands the removal of small amounts of material. To do that requires very sharp knives or chisels. A grinding wheel will do your sharpening quickly and efficiently.

Spoke shave. This is a small plane with ears for handles, but unlike a plane, you draw it toward you when you want it to shave the wood. It is an excellent tool for any close work.

Craft knife. This has replaceable blades which you can find in a variety of shapes. The minute you go near a piece of wood veneer you will need a craft knife, to say nothing of the thousands of other uses you can find for it.

Glue injector. This is really a metal syringe that is filled with glue. The glue is forced through a blunt needle that can be poked into tight corners or under the edges of raised veneer or plastic laminate.

Hand saws. Given either a radial arm or a bench saw plus a saber saw, you hardly need any hand saws. If you do not have access to any of the power tools, you will probably end up owning a ripsaw, backsaw, crosscut, keyhole and coping saws. Each has special capabilities.

Miter box. You can make a wooden miter box and use it with your backsaw. Better still, buy a metal version with a rotating frame for the saw blade that allows you to cut wood at virtually any angle you wish.

Finish Work

Swab sticks. Sold in drugstores for cleaning out your ears, these are perfect for picking out dirt and debris in tight places.

Rubbing blocks. These are like sanding blocks, but are a little more flexible. You can buy some sanding blocks with a padded piece that is removed for sanding and put on for rubbing. You can also make a rubbing block with pieces of felt or hard rubber.

Shellac sticks. You can buy these singly or in sets, in a full range of wood colors. They are melted and pushed into cracks or scratches to hide the mars in wood.

Spatula. Get one with about a ½″-wide blade. It is ideal for applying all kinds of patching materials including wood putty, plastic wood and particularly shellac sticks.

Alcohol lamp. This will heat the blade of your spatula or putty knife without leaving soot on the blade. The hot blade is then rubbed against a shellac stick until it is covered with material that you can apply to the wood.

SPECIALTY TOOLS AND MATERIALS

If you are doing only minor repairs to wood and wood finishes, you have no need for any of the tools listed here. But take on even a minor upholstery job, and you will need a good many of the following.

Tack hammer. This is a must for all sorts of tasks, not the least of which is pounding home upholstery tacks.

Staple gun. Sometimes this can be used instead of a hammer and tacks. It is relatively expensive ($10 to $15), but a good one will handle two or three different sizes of staples. You will get your money's worth from it.

Shears. Buy good-quality steel shears in a size that is large enough to handle heavy materials. If you are left-handed get a left-handed pair, or all that rough material will give you some painful blisters. It is not a bad idea to have a smaller pair for lighter materials.

Webbing stretcher. This is a necessity for pulling webbing and sometimes other fabrics taut before you tack or staple them to the frame of a chair or sofa.

Webbing. A roll of burlap or plastic used for seat and back reinforcement, this is also good for holding springs in place and numerous other tasks.

Assorted tacks and nails. The only time nails are used in good furniture is to hold upholstery in place. Buy the kind of tacks or nails you need for each job; eventually you will build up a reservoir of left-over fasteners.

Heavy flax cord. This should be ⅛" in diameter and is used to fasten together springs, webbing and other parts of upholstery.

Small metal straps. These are used for fastening the base of springs to the wood frame.

Padding. You will encounter times when you need the foam and/or cotton versions.

Muslin. This goes over the padding in furniture and acts as a protector between the stuffing and cover material.

Upholstery needles. Sometimes you can use standard sewing needles, but since upholstery tends to be made of heavier fabrics, you'll generally need these heavy needles. They are sold in both straight and curved versions— invest in both.

Upholstery fabrics. Fabrics used for upholstery are heavy and therefore expensive. Unless you are getting into a great deal of reupholstering, you will probably want to buy only what you need when you need it, even though it may be cheaper to buy an entire bolt of cloth.

Reseating

The techniques of weaving seats and backs require no special tools other than a strong pair of hands. You will, however, need the proper materials, which are available at any chair-seating or specialty store. Caning is the process of weaving rattan cane strips through holes in a frame edge. Rushing is the process of weaving natural rush or a substitute around the outer edges of a frame.

Cane. This is the shiny bark from the rattan palm which has been cut into narrow strips as long as 20', or is already woven into an open network before you buy it. Buy real rattan. Sugar and bamboo canes are also sold, but they are not really strong enough for chair seating. Plastic cane is strong enough, but hardly looks authentic.

Rush. Natural rush is made by soaking and then twisting leaves together into tight, weavable lengths. Around the month of August you could wander into the nearest swamp and make your own rush. Cut some cattails with long, narrow leaves that are about 7' long. Then pull off the leaves and air them for about three weeks in a dry, dark, breezy room. When they are dry, twist them together into weavable lengths.

You can purchase several kinds of equally good rush substitutes in continuous lengths. Paper twist as well as several kinds of synthetic fibers are now manufactured in seat-length spools, balls and hanks. You can also use tough string or thin rope.

Splints. Long, thin strips of ash, hickory or rattan splints are often referred to as reeds. They are woven together to make chair seats or backs.

Painted Decorative Finishes

Achieving a decorative finish with paint requires some natural artistic talent and a knowledge of the tricks that work. The basic techniques are described in Chapter 5, but the materials you will need include the following.

JAPAN COLORS

You can buy these at practically any art supply store. They are sold in both tubes and small cans. The basic colors which can be combined to make any hue or shade you wish are:

Liberty red medium
Signcraft red
Chrome yellow light
Green medium (coach paint)
Green light (coach paint)
Raw umber
Burnt umber
Raw sienna
Burnt sienna
French yellow ochre
Lampblack

You can use white poster paint with any of the japan colors to achieve lighter shades.

OTHER MATERIALS

In addition to the basic paints listed above, you'll need the following items.
Solvents and diluters. Turpentine, denatured alcohol, benzene, soybean oil and japan drier all fall into this category. Buy them when you are choosing particular finish materials and colors, and know which you specifically need.
Brushes. You will need some high-quality natural bristle brushes, as well as the best artist's brushes you can find. Number 3 and #6 long-haired point sable artist's brushes are the two basic tools for decorating.
Palette knife. You need this for blending your colors. As you delve more and more into decorative finishes, you will undoubtedly discover all kinds of weird and wonderful ingredients that can be used to achieve different effects in a furniture finish. Buy and use them as you need them. They include lacquers, casein paste, ox gall, kaolin powder, India ink, aniline powders and a host of other obscure materials including gold leaf. (Gold leaf is not really obscure, but the current price of gold threatens to drive it out of existence.)

A Place to Work

Some home projects can be done anywhere, from a dusty attic to a damp cellar or unheated garage. Not so with furniture repair or restoration. You must have a warm, dust-free, dry place to do your work. Glue needs a warm environment in order to harden properly; varied temperature and moisture conditions will play havoc with any raw wood; varnishes, shellacs and paints will gather dust particles from the air as they are drying, and some of them will be busy collecting that debris for as long as 24 hours.

The place you choose as your work space can be in a heated basement, an extra room in your house, even the garage if it is warm enough. Wherever it is, remember that you must be able to control both the humidity and temperature, as well as the cleanliness of the air.

WORKBENCH

Into your work area should go an old-fashioned 18″- or 24″-wide workbench with plenty of storage space under, over and behind it. Perforated hardboard nailed to the wall behind the bench is an excellent medium for hanging all of your tools. There should be a cabinet for storing finishing materials, and a drawer for small tools and objects. Keep your nails, screws, dowels and other small what-nots in glass jars. You might nail a 2″×4″ board to the back edge of the bench to keep things from falling off it. You can also drill holes in the 2×4 to hold bits, brushes, screwdrivers, files, rasps and almost anything else that has a small handle.

WORK PLATFORM

Working with furniture resting on a normal workbench can create some problems in height; a chair seat becomes too high to get at, a bureau top is raised almost to the ceiling. A useful addition to your work space is a platform that measures about 3′ by 4′ and stands around 24″ high. You can build the platform from 2″×4″ stock and cover the top of its frame with a piece of ¾″ plywood, giving you an even surface to rest your furniture on as you work. The platform should be carefully constructed so that when it stands on the floor it is absolutely level in all directions. In other words, you may have a leg or two that is shorter than the others to make up for the slant in your workshop floor. You can also tack, or simply place, a piece of old rug on the platform so that the finish on the piece you are working with will not be marred or scratched.

The work platform is convenient for doing much of your repair work as well as for stripping and refinishing, particularly if you build it exactly high enough for you to work comfortably.

HOW IT'S PUT TOGETHER

Sooner or later it will become apparent to you that every material known to man is used in the manufacture of furniture. But glass, metal, plastic and paper represent but a small percentage of the material in furniture. The majority of pieces we use today are made as they have always been made—with wood.

Wood Basics

Even with the march of technology, wood remains the choice for most people because it is easily cut, shaped, fitted and joined, and it can be finished to a rich warmth and in hues that cannot be matched by any other material. Some woods are dense in their composition, others are porous. Some woods are soft, others hard. Some are light in color, others dark.

HARDWOODS AND SOFTWOODS

The capability to accurately identify which of the 25,000 different species a particular piece of wood belongs to requires the training of a scientist. This intricate technical information is reduced for most people to categorizing woods as "hardwoods" or "softwoods." It should be noted that the two categories are extremely broad; there are, for example, some hardwoods such as balsa that are decidedly softer than any of the softwoods.

A hardwood is any tree that bears flowers during each growing season and has broad leaves which it loses each year. As far as furniture making is concerned, the usual hardwoods are oak, walnut, cherry, birch, elm, mahogany, rosewood, hickory and ash. The softwoods are the evergreen trees, or conifers, such as pine, fir, spruce, cedar and redwood. These are all cone bearing and retain their greenery throughout the year.

When cabinetmakers select the woods they intend for making furniture they are looking for particular characteristics which include: *stability*—the ability of the wood to hold its shape without shrinking, swelling or warping; ease of *workability* when shaping, surfacing and finishing; *attractiveness,* which actually may include surface defects in the wood; suitable *strength* and attractive *grain;* and *availability.*

Hardwoods usually have all of the above qualities, while softwoods ordinarily lack some degree of stability, strength or attractive grain configurations. As a result, with the exception of the Colonial style, which has the "rustic" look of primitive furniture, the softwoods are usually used when the finished piece is to be painted.

PLYWOOD

Most people think of plywood in terms of the large 4′ × 8′ panels faced with pine or fir. Most people are also aware that plywood is a strong, water-resistant man-made material. It does have tremendous strength because each of the veneers, or layers, that make up a panel is glued with its grain running at right angles to the veneers above and below it.

But there are considerably more kinds of plywood than just the softwood panels. Many types are given face veneers made from oak, walnut, birch, maple and mahogany, making them ideal for the manufacture of handsome hardwood-veneered furniture.

HARDBOARD

Hardboard is manufactured by saturating wood fibers with resin and then pressurizing the mass under intense heat into the shape of panels. The result is a hard, even wood that has equal strength in all directions. Cabinetmakers have found it ideal for use in cabinet backs, dustcovers between shelves, and drawer bottoms. It is, therefore, a material to consider seriously whenever you need to replace any of the thin, unseen parts of casework.

Joinery: The Key to Assembling Wood

Wood is a natural bounty; but for all of its versatility and varieties, there are only 100 or so ways in which two or more pieces of wood can be effectively joined. These methods have been devised over the centuries and all have proven their worth with the passing of time. Moreover, no one has found any better ways of joining wood. Machines have been devised for making the joints more accurately, but there are no better joints than the ones mankind had thousands of years ago.

The essential element to effective furniture repair is a full understanding of wood joints and how they are assembled. It is not unusual to encounter a piece of furniture that is in such disrepair that the most propitious way of restoring it is to completely take it apart and then put it together again from scratch. But to disassemble the piece, you'd best understand how all of its parts are held together in the first place, or you are liable to break the wood rather than the joints.

The first thing to understand about any furniture joint is that it is most likely held together with glue. There may also be screws or, more likely, dowels inserted in the center of the joint to further strengthen it. The second thing you must know is how the joint is constructed. The surface may show a simple straight line between the two pieces of wood; never assume that that straight line is the only place the pieces meet. There may be several other matching surfaces buried inside the wood.

Butt Joints

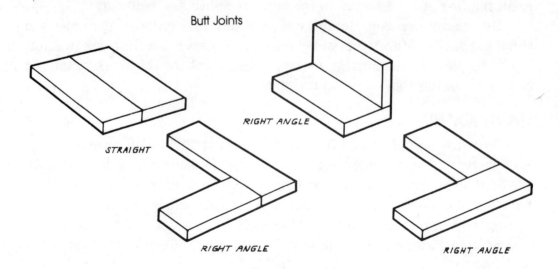

STRAIGHT

RIGHT ANGLE

RIGHT ANGLE

RIGHT ANGLE

BUTT JOINTS

These are, indeed, the joints formed when two pieces of wood simply butt together. However, the butt joint is inherently weak, and if you discover one in a piece of furniture, the matching parts are probably either backed by some other member, or there are screws or nails driven into the joints. If neither of these conditions is present, you can be pretty certain there is a dowel or two bridging the joint in the center of the wood.

LAP JOINTS

These are often used in cabinet or chair rails to join two pieces of wood so that their overlap is no thicker than a single member. The lap joint is made by cutting a notch in both parts that is no deeper than half the thickness of the wood. The two notches are then glued together, with the adhesive applied to all surfaces that meet. Fasteners might be driven through the joint, but most likely it will only be glued.

RABBET JOINTS

These joints are made by cutting notches in the edges of two pieces of wood. The rabbet might be used to hold together two boards side by side. More often they appear in the top and bottom edges of casework sides, holding the top and/or bottom of the casework to the sides; sometimes rabbets are used to inset the backs of cabinets. The rabbet may be cut from one or both of the two joining pieces, but either way it is not a holding joint. It must at least have a strong adhesive to keep it together and is often strengthened by nails, screws or dowels.

DADO JOINTS

Dadoes are the workhorses of cabinetmaking. A trough or groove (dado) is cut out of one member, just wide enough to accept the edge of the second member. If the fit is tight enough, the two pieces of wood will stay together by themselves, but the usual practice is to also put glue in the dado.

Dadoes are used anytime two pieces of wood form a right angle, which is why shelves are often dadoed into their vertical supports. But cabinetmakers have developed some sneaky versions of the simple dado, beginning with the blind (or stopped) dado. Thus you can look at the front edge of a

Lap Joints

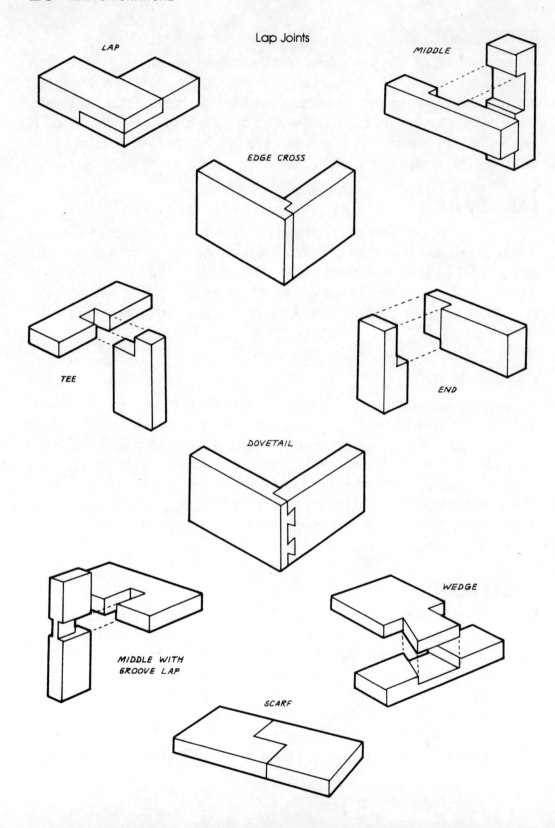

LAP

MIDDLE

EDGE CROSS

TEE

END

DOVETAIL

MIDDLE WITH GROOVE LAP

WEDGE

SCARF

Rabbet Joints

Dado Joints

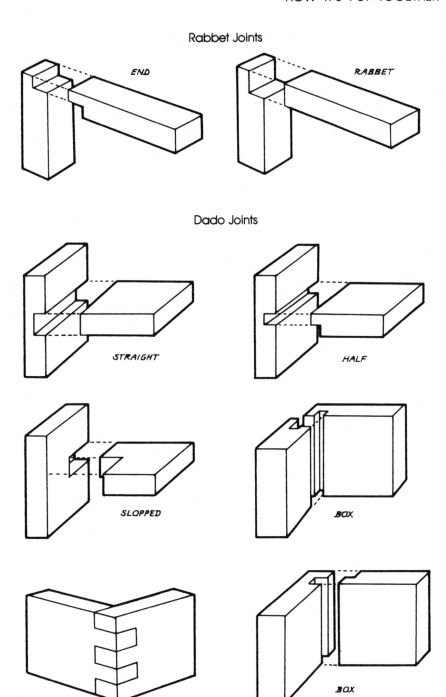

Mortise-and-Tenon Joints

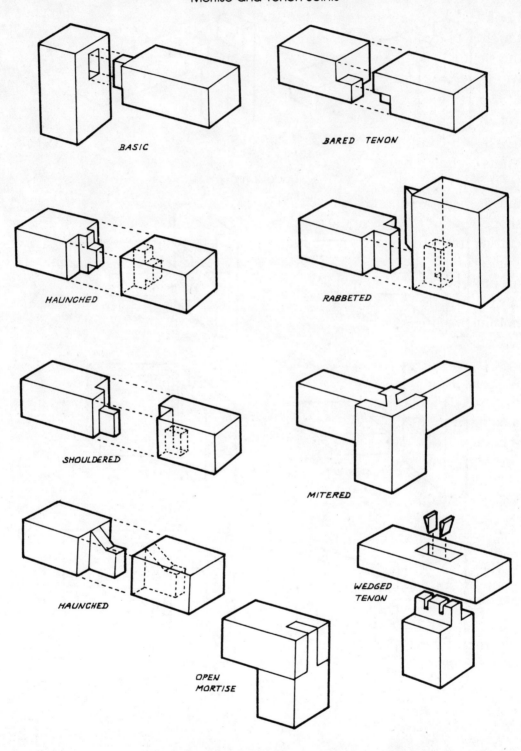

BASIC

BARED TENON

HAUNCHED

RABBETED

SHOULDERED

MITERED

HAUNCHED

OPEN MORTISE

WEDGED TENON

shelf case and think the shelves are merely butted against their uprights. Look at the sides of the furniture and also feel along the tops and bottoms of the shelves for any sign of nails or screws. If you find none, it is possible that the shelf is held in place with dowels. More likely, a dado stops an inch or two from the front edge of the vertical members.

MORTISE-AND-TENON JOINTS

These are considered the most dependable, strongest and best of all the joints. Whole bridges have been built with nothing but mortise-and-tenon joints—no glue or fasteners at all. The joint consists of a square hole (the mortise) cut out of one member and a corresponding square peg (the tenon) shaped out of the end of the other piece. The tenon is usually made first by cutting down the board end to between a quarter and one-half the original thickness of the wood. Then the mortise is drilled and chiseled out to fit around the tenon. There must be considerable precision in measuring and cutting a mortise and tenon and that takes some practice, but there is nothing like this particular joint to guarantee that the rails of a chair or table will stay together forever.

Beware—the surface crack that shows in a mortise-and-tenon joint looks as if the two pieces were put together with a butt joint. If they were, they will definitely have dowels between them. Two dowels in a butt joint is a configuration considered equal in strength to a mortise and tenon and is infinitely easier to assemble, which is why so many modern furniture makers prefer to use dowels.

DOVETAIL JOINTS

These are the Cadillacs of joinery. For most of the 5,000 years since they were invented by the Egyptians they were made by hand, but today cabinetmakers can use a router bit and dovetail template, which will cut a joint for an average-size drawer corner in less than 60 seconds. So the dovetail remains in favor. It consists of an intricate system of interlocking flared tenons and, if made properly, needs nothing but itself to stay together. Even so, dovetails are glued, particularly when you find them in a drawer assembly. They are never nailed or screwed.

Dovetail Joints

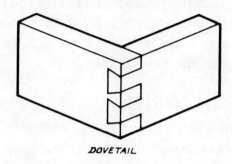

DOVETAIL

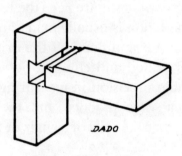

DADO

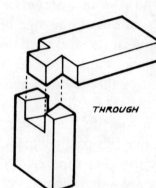

THROUGH

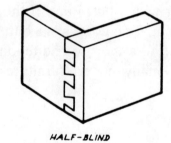

HALF-BLIND

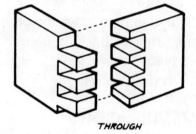

THROUGH

HIDDEN

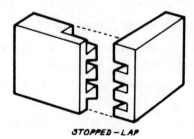

STOPPED-LAP

Miter Joints

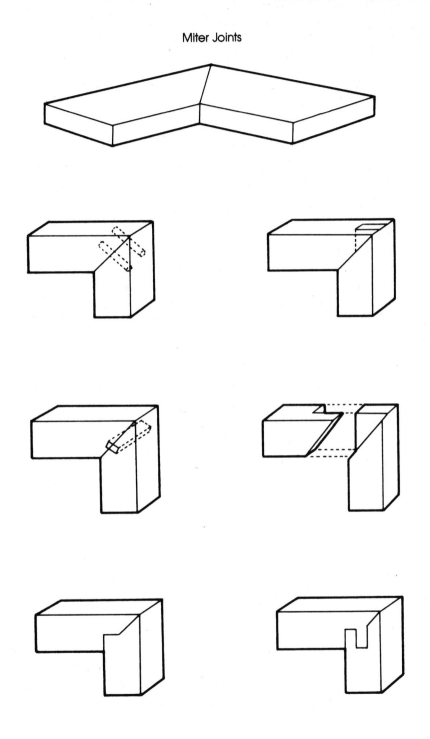

MITER JOINTS

These are actually angled butt joints and have no more holding power than any other butt. Traditionally, the miter is cut at a 45° angle, but technically it can be anything other than 90° (at which point it becomes a butt joint). Miters are usually found in moldings or cabinet face frames, where they are backed by some other portion of the furniture. If a miter is backed, its members can be fastened to the supporting parts for strength, and the joint is merely glued. If the miter requires added strength, nails or screws are driven through its outside edges or, most likely, held together with dowels.

There are dozens of other joints, but all of them really are combinations or variations of the joints described above. It is best to assume that the joints in any furniture piece are not what they appear to be. If the joint is hidden from view on the underside or back of a cabinet, it will usually be the least decorative and strongest joint possible. Wherever people will see it, the joint may be equally strong but will also be more decorative, or at least more complicated. For example, you might have a frame assembled with mortise-and-tenon joints, but the visible side of the frame has also been mitered.

Most of the joints that need repair work are the ones that are not complex enough to offer holding power of their own, other than to present more gluing surfaces than a simple butt joint. However, if you decide that the furniture you are restoring would be stronger if you completely disassembled and reglued it, you are going to have to take apart all joints.

Taking Furniture Apart

Assume nothing. Closely inspect the furniture you are disassembling. Look at each of the joints and try to discern what kind they are. Poke around the cracks with a knife blade to determine the condition of the glue. If the furniture has legs, stand it on something level and rock it to see if the legs are even or if the frame is twisted in some way. Locate all the loose joints—the ones that appear as if they will come apart with a minimum of effort on your part. Look carefully to see if there are any missing members. Search the surface of the wood for cracks, holes, gouges, dents, any defects. If the piece has a veneer, examine it minutely for bubbles, blisters, cracks and loose edges. Note any members that are warped. Look at doors and drawers for loose joints or warping.

When you are satisfied that you have a good idea of all the defects, begin your disassembly by removing all of the hardware, screws and nails you can locate. The fasteners may be hidden under wooden plugs or wood putty which must be dug out first.

Begin with the easy joints. With luck, you can pull them apart. If that fails, tap them with a mallet. Each joint that you take apart will give you a clue to the kind of joint used in opposite members. If the rail between the front legs of a chair is mortised and tenoned, you can be pretty sure the back legs are held together the same way. You can be pretty sure, but not dead certain, so continue to go cautiously. If your mallet fails to loosen a joint, minutely examine the members again for any hidden fasteners you may have missed. If there are none, try prying the joint apart with a knife blade or chisel. As a last resort, soak the joint in warm water—most glues dissolve in water or acetone. But if you have reached the extreme of using water, consider whether it is really necessary to dismantle the joint at all, particularly if all you intend to do is reglue and reassemble it.

When you have removed all the hidden fasteners and broken open all the glued joints, you will have reduced your furniture to a pile of odd-shaped pieces of lumber. Now the real task of repairing and restoring can begin.

3

FUNDAMENTAL FIXING

Frames exist as the backbone of any chair, sofa, table or casework, and are assembled from separate pieces joined at various angles so that they provide support for each other. In a simple, solid-seat kitchen chair, the frame is not very complicated. But look at a Windsor chair and just for fun, count the two dozen or more separate members that make up the unit. Individually, each part is small in diameter and has no particular strength. But when all those pieces are assembled so that they support each other, they form a durable structure. That structure has a great many glued joints, any of which can work loose and require repair work.

Casework is the general term for cabinets, bureaus, chests, desks and bookshelves. Their basic structure is that of a box. Their frames may be either the solid wood pieces that form the top, sides and back, or a skeleton of rails that support each other as well as provide a backing for thin side panels. The panels are often made of an inexpensive wood which is covered with an exotic veneer, but they can also be pieces of solid cabinet wood. Case furniture often incorporates shelves as well as drawers and doors; they in turn are held in place by some system of rails and stiles, which itself becomes a frame.

The Ground Rules

When a joint in a piece of furniture wood comes apart or a member of the frame splits or breaks, you have numerous approaches toward rendering a durable repair. In some instances you will have to improvise, since each piece of furniture may have been assembled in a slightly different manner. There are, however, some general procedures to follow whenever you are dealing with the wooden parts of any furniture.

Always examine the entire piece before you make any repairs. The loose joint that has turned your attention to repairing the furniture may be only a symptom rather than a cause. Chair arms, for instance, usually get loose because the back has come loose first. Fixing the arm will do you no good whatsoever unless you also reglue the back.

Try to make all repairs in the style of the original construction. If a leg was put together with dowels, use dowels to reassemble it. If the rails of a table were mortise and tenoned, use a mortise and tenon.

Try to avoid driving nails into furniture. Nails will not only weaken the wood, but are likely to split it as well. Besides, nails do not hold wood together very well.

If you must use screws, always drill a pilot hole first. In most instances, the wood you will encounter in furniture is a hardwood. If you drive a screw into it without a pilot hole, besides developing blisters on your hands, you will split the wood.

2101708

The Dry Run

Whenever you are reassembling furniture, always practice first. Fit the parts together without applying any glue, just to make absolutely certain that all the parts do indeed fit together properly. More importantly, you want to teach yourself how you are going to proceed during the assembly and make certain you have all the proper tools on hand.

If you are regluing a chair, for example, put all the pieces together and hold them that way with some clamps. When you remove the clamps, leave them open to their proper widths and place them carefully on a workbench near where you will be using them. As you apply glue to each joint, all you'll need to do is pick up the correct clamp, position it, and tighten it with a twist of your wrist. Some glues, such as the acrylics, set within five minutes, so you will not have much time to get your joint into proper alignment and clamp it; if you have to waste that time opening the jaws of your clamps, chances are you will not have time to properly assemble the joint.

Repairs with Wedges, Dowels and Shims

Anytime you have to fill a hole that must then accept a screw, fill it with wood. This means using wedges, dowels or shims.

WEDGES

You can make any size wedge by chiseling off the edge of a piece of scrap wood. Cut the wedge so that it is at least 1/16″ longer than the depth of the hole, and coat it with glue. Also put glue in the hole, then tap the wedge as far as it will go. When the glue has dried, sand the top of the wedge flush with the surface around it.

DOWELS

Dowels are used to fill round holes. If the wood is ragged, it sometimes pays to drill the hole a little larger so that it is smooth and the dowel can fit into it snugly. However you arrive at it, the hole should be exactly the same diameter as the dowel you put into it. Glue is applied to both the dowel and its hole, and the dowel is then tapped into position. Like wedges, dowels should extend above the surface of the wood a fraction of an inch and then be sanded flush after the glue dries.

SHIMS

The hinges you find in most cabinet doors, on the leaves of drop-leaf tables—or anywhere on fine pieces of furniture—have been recessed in mortises cut out of the wood that holds them. Years of wear can tear the wood around the hinge screws and enlarge their holes; a door can warp and refuse to open and close properly; the hinge bed can just plain wear down. The safest, most durable method of repairing a damaged mortise is with shims.

A shim is a thin piece of wood. You can cut one from any wood that is the proper thickness, or chisel a piece from a thicker piece of stock. You can also use cardboard or any other material, since the object is to fill in the mortise just enough so that you can replace the hinge over it. If you simply want to fill the mortise and position the hinges elsewhere, the shim you use should be the same kind of wood as the stile or rail it is inserted in and, of course, be thicker than a normal shim.

If a mortise is torn and its screw holes have split or become enlarged, always fill the holes with dowels before you insert your shim. You might also need to sand the bottom of the mortise so that it is flat enough to act as a proper gluing surface. Now cut a shim that will fit snugly into the mortise and raise the bottom of the hole to the proper depth for the hinge. Apply glue to the mortise and the bottom of the shim, then clamp the shim in the hole until the glue has dried. Only when the glue is dry should you attempt to put the hinge back in its mortise.

Shims are also used to fill in joints that have come apart but not loosened, to level shelves and in any situation where the surface of the wood must be brought up to a particular level. Always coat them with glue before inserting them into the wood.

Hinge Repairs

You will encounter a confounding array of hinges if you begin to take notice of them on every piece of furniture you see. There are pivot hinges and decorative face hinges, standard hinges, split ones, and so on and on and on. No matter what its shape or size (piano hinges can be ½″ wide and as much as 8′ long), the hinge must in some way be attached to the two pieces of wood it bridges. That attachment is almost universally made with screws. And therein lie all of the problems that arise with hinges.

In most cases hinge screws are not particularly large, but there may be as many as 192 of them (as in the 8′ piano hinge). Resting on the strength of those screws can be the considerable weight of a table leaf, a wooden door or a chestful of objects. Moreover, every time the hinge is opened or closed, the pressure on the screws increases and shifts position, pulling at the screws which in turn tear at the wood around them. The screws might bend or break; more often, the wood around them gives way and they come loose from holes that have become too large to hold them. Sometimes the wood between screw holes splits.

Removing the hinge screws can have a weakening effect. A hinge may have to be taken off so that other parts of the furniture can be repaired; it is best to remove them before applying a finish to the wood, for example. There can be any number of valid reasons for taking the screws out of a hinge, but every time you do so, be very careful not to damage the hinge or mar the wood around it. And before you replace the screws, examine the wood in the hinge mortise closely. If the screw holes look as if they are too large, fill them with glue and dowels, then drill new pilot holes for the screws. In some cases, you can get away with just using a fatter or longer screw, but you will risk splitting the wood. You can also buy a different hinge with its screw holes in different positions, in which case the old screw holes should be filled before new holes are bored in the wood.

If the wood between screw holes is split, pry the wood apart just enough to work a strong glue into the break, then clamp your repair until the glue dries. Use the strongest glue you can find—an acrylic, epoxy or aliphatic.

DOOR HINGES

The most common problems that arise with doors are usually solved at the hinges. It may be that the door has swollen and its edges must be planed down. But before you do that, look at the hinges. Are they all mortised so that every hinge leaf lies flush with the wood surrounding it? If not, shim the leaf until it is level with the wood surface. It *must* be level, with both ends equally deep in the wood. Hinges normally work in pairs; if the barrels are not aligned, they will cause the door to open and close with difficulty, if at all. If the top half of the closing edge of a door (the hingeless side) rubs against its frame, shim out the bottom hinge. If the bottom edge of the door rubs, shim the top hinge.

If the top of a door rubs against its frame, shim the bottom hinge; if the bottom rubs, shim the top hinge.

INSTALLING HINGES

It is not an easy task to install a set of hinges. The work itself is simple enough, but mistakes can crop up at almost every step of the process, even when you are being extremely careful. The following procedure applies to any hinge installment, whether it is for the front door of your house or the lid of a veneered cabinet.

1. Carefully align the two elements you are hinging. Make absolutely certain you have the pieces in the exact positions you want them. If you can clamp or in some other manner lock them together temporarily, do it.

2. Decide where you want the hinges to be placed. When you have them exactly where you want them, tape them to the wood with masking or gummed tape. If you are installing a typical double-leaf hinge, the barrels

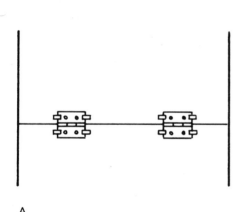

A

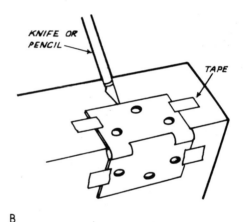

B

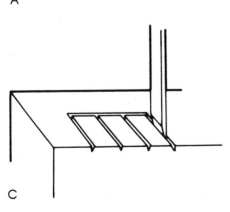

C

To install hinges: (A) If possible, tape hinges in their exact positions before you do any mortising or screwing. (B) Trace the hinge leaves if the hinge is to be mortised; mark the screw holes if the hinge is to be flush-mounted. (C) With a chisel held vertically, cut the outline of the mortise, then make some cuts across the grain of the wood.

that hold the hinge pins should butt between the edges of the wood. Be sure that the entire length of the barrel is touching the edges of the wood at all points. Be certain that both the hinges are parallel by setting them against a common edge of the wood—and pray that the edge is straight.

3. With the hinge taped in place, trace the leaf with a pencil, unless you are flush-mounting the hinge. If you are not submerging the hinge in a mortise, simply mark the screw holes and drill them. If you are mortising the hinge you can outline both leaves with a pencil and then remove the tape.

4. Using a chisel held straight up and down with the beveled side toward the inside of the mortise, cut along the inside of your three pencil lines. Theoretically, each cut will be no deeper than the thickness of the hinge leaf. But the chances of your making half a dozen chisel cuts all exactly 3/32″ deep are practically nil. Just do the best you can by being careful to align the chisel blade exactly along the outline. When you have cut around the mortise, make several more cuts across the grain of the wood to divide the mortise into sections that you can remove more easily.

5. Now comes the hard part. You do not want to chisel the mortise so deeply that the hinge leaf lies below the surface of the wood or the hinge will not close properly. You will rarely be chiseling more than 1/8″ of wood, but you have probably cut deeper than that with your chisel. When you are all finished, the mortise must be uniformly deep so that the hinge will lie flat in its bed. The best you can do is excavate the mortise using short, very shallow cuts of your chisel and trying not to gouge the wood; then sand the bed with an abrasive.

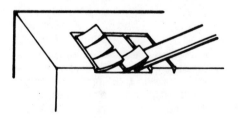 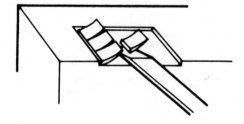

Carefully chip out the mortise so that its bed is flat and parallel to the surface of the frame or rail.

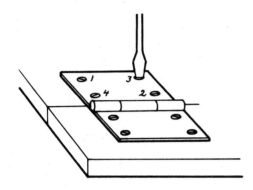

The screws in a hinge should be tightened alternately to insure that the leaf is bedded evenly.

6. You can fit in your hinges as soon as their mortises are cut and smoothed to the proper depth. If the hinge fits tightly and does not move, fine. If it is able to move around in the mortise, tape it in place *with its barrel snugly against the edge of the wood.* Then drill pilot holes for the hinge screws.

All of the screws in a hinge leaf should now be tightened. Start each screw in its hole, and then alternate tightening them until each is completely seated. If you have drilled your pilot holes in the exact center of the screw holes in the hinge, driven the screws exactly perpendicular into the wood and tightened the screws alternately, and the tape has held the hinge in place, the barrel of the hinge will remain against the edge of the wood. If all of the barrel is not touching wood by the time you are finished, the hinge is out of line. Remove the screws, fill the screw holes with dowels and start all over again.

7. When you have attached the hinges to, let's say, a door, stand the door in place with the free hinge leaves open so that you can mark their position on the door frame. Whether you are hanging a door or not, the two pieces connected by the hinges should be carefully aligned before you mark the mortise positions on the unmortised member. Once the mortises are marked, chisel them out and smooth the beds with sandpaper.

8. Assemble the two pieces by inserting the free leaves in their mortises, then recheck their alignment. If it is correct, drill one hole in one of the mortises and install one screw. If the units are still aligned, place one screw in the other hinge. Work the hinges to be certain the pieces open and close properly and are correctly aligned. If they are not, remove one of the screws (or both if you must) and reposition the hinges until you have the correct alignment. Only then do you put in the remaining screws.

Never drill a pilot hole with a bit that is too large or too small for the screw that will go into it.

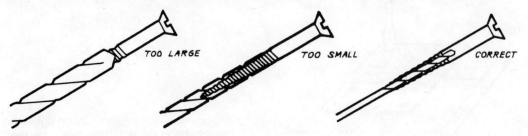

Tips for Drilling and Screwing

You can drill holes in hardwood furniture with either a hand drill or a ratchet brace. An electric drill is not only faster and easier, but it has some useful accessories such as depth gauges, countersinks and screwdriver blades, all of which will take the drudgery out of removing or installing screws.

No matter what kind of drill you are using, there are some precautions that should be observed whenever you are boring holes in a good piece of furniture. Be careful to fully support or brace the work. Whenever possible, take the time to punch a small centering hole in the wood, using a nail or awl, so that the drill will not slip as it first touches the wood. Pilot holes for screws should be no larger than the diameter of the screw shaft minus its threads. To determine the proper size bit to use, match it against the threaded portion of the screw and hold them both up to the light. If you can see the screw threads above and below the bit, the bit is the correct diameter. If you cannot see the threads, select a smaller-diameter bit.

When you are driving screws, it is important that you use a screwdriver blade that fits snugly into the screw slot and does not overhang the head of the screw. If the blade is too thick or wide for the screw slot, you will not be able to get proper torque as you turn the screw. If the blade is too small for the slot, it will slip and not only gouge the wood around the screw, but chew up the slot as well. On occasion, you can repair a screw slot by filing it with a small file or making it deeper with a hacksaw blade. It is easier, of course, to just throw away the screw and get a new one.

There are three ways in which you can free a "frozen" screw, short of cutting it off with a hacksaw. If a screw refuses to loosen, tighten it a quarter-turn or half-turn. Then loosen it. Tighten it again. Loosen it again. Continue tightening and loosening until the screw comes free. Alternatively, place a narrow screwdriver blade against one side of the screw slot; hold the blade at a low angle and tap it with a hammer until the screw loosens. When all else fails, heat the screw head with the tip of a dry (not steam) iron or a soldering gun, then let the metal cool. Heat will expand the screw. As the metal cools it will shrink and should free itself from whatever is holding it.

Glue Blocks

Turn your best dining room chair upside down, and look at the corners under its seat. You will find triangular pieces of wood glued and/or screwed or doweled into each of the corners near the legs. You will probably find other, similar blocks of wood positioned at any juncture that may have to endure inordinate stress. If you look under any good piece of furniture, you will find glue blocks everywhere, including under drawer bottoms.

Glue blocks are not put in furniture because some cranky Old World cabinetmaker had a whim to stick them on. They have a definite purpose: to keep the piece from wobbling. They force the joints they stand behind to remain square, and provide added gluing surfaces to reinforce joints. Modern furniture makers have found that they can turn out their products without glue blocks and save the cost of materials and labor. But their furniture will not last long, nor can it withstand much of the normal stress and strain that furniture must sustain. Anytime you are repairing or restoring a piece of furniture and notice that there are no glue blocks, add them, particularly to the leg-to-base and base-to-back-to-arm joints. It is best if you make your glue blocks from hardwood, but it is not mandatory. Simply glue them in place, or glue and screw them or, best of all, glue them and hold them in place with dowels.

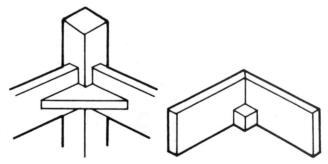

Some variations of the glue block. It can be any shape you wish as long as it fits snugly into the corner it is supporting.

Doweling for Strength

A dowel is a wooden, plastic or metal peg that is used to assemble and strengthen joints in furniture. Engineers have proven that two dowels inserted into the middle of a standard butt joint make that joint equal in strength to a mortise and tenon. Dowels are always used with glue and are preferable to nails, screws, bolts, brackets or any other metal fastener, all of which can damage the wood around them. So if you plan to do any skillful furniture repair, you must learn to be adroit at doweling; fortunately, there is nothing very complicated about dowels or their application.

You can insert a dowel between practically any two pieces of wood that are forming a joint. You can also put them in the middle of a split piece of wood that you are gluing together. You can drill a hole large enough for a dowel all the way through two pieces of wood, coat the dowel with glue and insert it—but its ends will be visible. That is quite acceptable in cases where you want the decorative effect of visible dowel ends, or in hidden parts of furniture. Most of the time, however, you will want to submerge your dowels inside a joint and make them invisible. To do so takes some precision drilling, but that's about all.

DRILLING DOWEL HOLES

As a rule of thumb, the diameter of the dowel you use should be no more than one-half the thickness of the wood it is to enter. As a second rule of thumb, whenever possible use at least two dowels—more if there is

(Right) A dowel should be no more than half the thickness of the wood it enters, and should be placed with as much wood around it as possible.

(Below) The best dowels are made of hardwood, but the plastic and softwood versions are adequate for most repairs. You can buy plastic dowels that form a right angle.

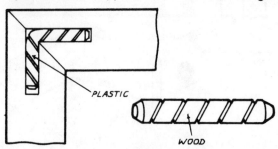

PLASTIC

WOOD

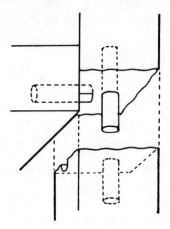

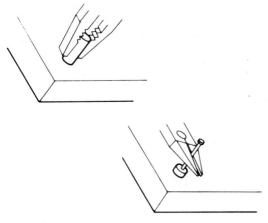

Two ways of removing a dowel.

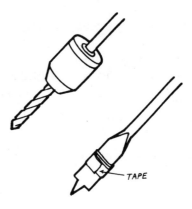

_TAPE

If you do not have a depth gauge for your drill (above left), wrap adhesive tape around the blade at the depth you want to drill.

space—in every joint. The dowel should go no deeper into either side than two-thirds of the combined thickness of the wood. In other words, if you assemble two pieces of wood each ¾" thick, the dowel should be 1" long.

Drilling the first half of a dowel hole is easy. Measure to the center of the wood, mark it and drill _straight_ into the wood. Make sure that your drill enters the wood at exactly a right angle. If you can use a drill press or a drill stand you are guaranteed of going into the wood vertically, but if you have to drill freehand all you can do is be as careful as possible.

Insert a doweling pin into the hole you have drilled. Now assemble the joint. Make sure the pieces are absolutely aligned in all directions, and then press them against each other. The pin in the doweling center will mark the center of the hole in the undrilled side of the joint. Now drill the hole in that side. Again, take great care not to drill any deeper than you need to, and to keep your drill bit entering the wood at a right angle.

In theory, you should now be able to insert the dowel in its holes and it will bridge the joint. If your drilling has been a little askew or not deep enough, drill a little deeper or widen the hole. If the hole gets too big you can stuff it with pieces of wood, but a better repair by far is to glue a dowel in the hole and saw it off flush with the wood. When the glue hardens, redrill the dowel hole.

PREPARING SMOOTH DOWELS

You can purchase 100 grooved and cut dowels for a dollar or so, if you can find them (not every lumberyard sells them). If you cannot find them, you can buy 3'-long dowel sticks, in diameters of ⅛" to 1", from most hardware stores, and cut them yourself. The diameters most often used in furniture repair are ¼", 5⁄16", ⅜" and ½".

Each dowel should be cut about ⅛" shorter than the combined depths of its two dowel holes. Both ends should be comfered, that is, tapered slightly, and a 1⁄16"-deep slot must be cut along the length of the dowel to allow excess glue to escape from the holes. You can cut the slot with a saw by holding the dowel in a vise. You can also use the serrated jaws of a pair of pliers to crimp the length of the dowel, which will make it look kind of like an elongated toothed gear. These indentations will allow excess glue to escape from the holes and squeeze between the edges of the joint, where you can wipe if off the wood.

TAKING OUT DOWELS

Most of the repairs you will make during the course of furniture restoration will involve reinforcing joints; fixing broken legs, arms, backs or wings; and strengthening broken or split seats and rails. Usually these repairs involve fixing, replacing or adding dowels. In many cases, when you examine the open joint you will find that half the dowel is still firmly imbedded in its hole and there is nothing you need to do about it except clean and reglue the exposed side. But there are times when it is best to remove the old dowel entirely and replace it with a new dowel. The following are a couple of accepted ways to get a broken or unwanted dowel out of its hole socket.

If the dowel is worn or broken, try gripping it with pliers and twisting, then pulling it. Take care that you do not exert so much force that you break the dowel to the point where you can no longer get a grip on it. If pliers do not give you enough leverage, try nail pullers; avoid prying around the base with a screwdriver or knife blade. You could chew up the hole and enlarge it too much to be reused.

If the dowel is broken off so that you can't get a grip on it, drill. Use a bit size that is exactly the diameter of the dowel—most likely you will need a spade bit. Go straight into the center of the socket, and avoid drilling any deeper than the depth of the socket. You can assume that the socket is no more than two-thirds of the thickness of the thinnest wood it enters; mark that depth on your bit by wrapping a piece of masking tape around the blade. Even with this precaution, drill carefully and watch for any change in the color of wood coming out of the hole, which sometimes tells you that you are through the dowel and into the furniture itself.

PUTTING IN DOWELS

Once the old dowel is removed, both of its sockets must be cleaned of all debris and old glue. Cleaning out a 5/16″-diameter hole requires a narrow tool such as a screwdriver, an old knife blade or a small file. New glue will not adhere to old glue, so this cleaning chore is a mandatory procedure, tiresome as it may be. When you have cleaned as much as you can, sand the insides of the holes by rolling a piece of sandpaper around the end of a pencil and rotating it in the sockets.

When the sockets are clean, insert your new dowel and fit the joint together. All matching surfaces should meet, so the faces of the joint itself must also be cleaned of old glue and sanded smooth. If the dowel is too long to allow the joining surfaces to make complete contact, either shorten the dowel or drill its sockets deeper.

When everything fits properly, assemble the clamps you plan to use to keep the joint together and set their jaws to the proper widths. Now apply glue to all of the gluing surfaces—put it in the sockets and on the dowel, and smear it evenly over the matching surfaces of the joint. Assemble and clamp the joint.

MORE DOWELS

The cabinetmakers who made your furniture knew what they were doing. You can assume, particularly with an antique, that their craftsmanship demanded the proper use of dowels, so there are only a few instances where new dowels need to be introduced. Usually, if a joint does not have a dowel to begin with, no dowel is necessary.

The one time the addition of dowels can be of great value is when you wish to reglue a broken rail or leg. Try to center your dowels so that there is as much wood around the socket as possible. Avoid drilling deeper into the

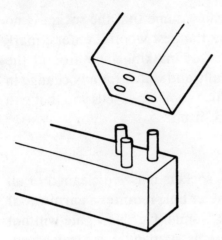

For a joint that will be subjected to twisting, such as the base of a chair leg, stagger the dowels to provide maximum resistance.

wood than you absolutely must or you will reach a point where you will weaken the wood. Since a dowel is strong and presumably resides in its sockets surrounded by an equally strong if not stronger glue, you are actually strengthening the wood surrounding a properly positioned dowel. But if you drill too near any of the member's outside surfaces, the added strength of the dowel is dissipated. In the case of a broken leg or rail, the diameter of the wood or the length of the break may be too small to allow more than one dowel to be inserted. Two dowels are always preferable if the member is to undergo much stress or strain; on the other hand, one dowel is better than none.

The addition of dowels, then, is a matter of common sense. If drilling holes in the wood will only weaken it, find some other way of bracing the member, such as using an extremely powerful glue. When you elect to add dowels, consider the amount of wood that will be left intact around the sockets, and do not overload the split with dowels you do not need. Not all dowels, of course, need to be hidden. You may find that at the back of a chair, for example, you can get away with drilling through the outside of two frame members and cutting the dowel flush with the wood. This would avoid taking the joint apart, which could entail disassembling several joints just to hide one dowel.

Gluing

Gluing is the preferred method of repairing furniture. The hide glues have been around for centuries and so has much of the furniture that was assembled with them. Today we have even stronger, faster drying glues that can be relied on for years of holding power, provided that they are used exactly according to the manufacturer's instructions. The advantage of glue is that it bonds wood to wood without weakening the construction as the insertion of a screw or nail will often do.

Whatever glue you use and no matter what the instructions tell you to do, there are some broad rules to bear in mind. The first of these is that new glue will not adhere to old glue. Old glue, no matter what kind it may be, has a hard, glossy surface that will keep new glue from getting into the fibers of the wood to form a solid bond. So you always have to clean the old glue from any surface that is to receive new glue. You can scrape it off with the sharp blade of a chisel or knife, but be careful not to gouge the wood. Your chances of just scraping instead of gouging will be improved if you keep your knife blade as vertical as possible when you work. When you have scraped away as much old glue as you can, sand the surfaces until they are smooth.

The purpose of any glue is to tightly bond together two or more surfaces. It is not within the capability of most glues to fill gaps between those surfaces. So the surfaces you are gluing should be even and sanded smooth and clean. When you are gluing raw wood, the glue is supposed to seep into the fibers and create a strong bond. If there is a finish material on the wood, the glue will have less opportunity to get down to the fibers, so always try to remove any foreign material from a gluing surface.

When gluing a joint, apply the glue liberally but evenly over every square inch of the gluing surfaces, and do not be concerned about getting too much glue into the joint. When the pieces of wood are brought together and clamped, excess glue will ooze out of the joint line. If it does not ooze out, break open the joint and add more glue—no seepage means there is not enough glue in the joint.

You must immediately wipe away excess glue with a damp cloth. Glue that has hardened on the surface of any wood cannot be sanded off; it can only be scraped. But the scraping may not get all of it off the wood. If you sand what is left you will not really remove it, you will only drive it deeper into the fibers where it may not be obvious—until you try to cover it with a finish material. At that point the finish will either not adhere to the glue area at all, or cause a glaringly light spot that even staining will not hide.

In almost every case, a rag dampened with water will clean away fresh glue; in a few rare instances, you will have to use acetone (nail polish remover) or add a detergent to the water. Read the label on the glue can. It will tell you what the solvent for the glue is; if it does not tell you anything specific, you can assume that plain water is sufficient.

Finally, there is the matter of clamping time. Nearly every glue except contact cement requires a period of time when the joint is clamped together while the glue hardens. The clamping time for hot melt glue is 60 seconds, so you might as well ignore your clamps and just hold the wood in place. Other glues require anything from five minutes to 24 hours to harden, but ignore all that and just assume that whatever you glue should remain in clamps at least overnight. The more time you give your glue to harden, the better the bond will be and the longer your repair will last.

THE REHEARSAL

Whenever you glue anything you are in the process of assembling, which has a centuries-old procedure. Following this process practically guarantees a successful repair. The procedure amounts to planning what you are going to do and then doing it, and it goes like this:

1. Clean and sand all of the surfaces to be glued.

2. Assemble all of the joints you intend to glue. Minutely examine each joint to make absolutely certain that all gluing surfaces come together at all points and every member is precisely aligned.

3. Set all of your clamps. If, for example, you are putting together an entire chair, get all of the joints together and hold them there with your clamps. When you are finished, you should be able to pick up the chair and carry it around without losing any parts.

4. Now remove the clamps. Open each one just enough to get it off the joint it's holding and place it on your workbench as close as possible to where you will need it. Leave the clamps open and ready to be used.

5. By the time you have disassembled the project, you will have learned which joints you need to glue first and how you can best clamp them. Now mix only as much glue as you will need to complete the job.

6. Glue, assemble and clamp each joint. Immediately wipe off all excess glue with a damp rag. When all of the joints are glued and clamped, go to bed and forget the project until tomorrow.

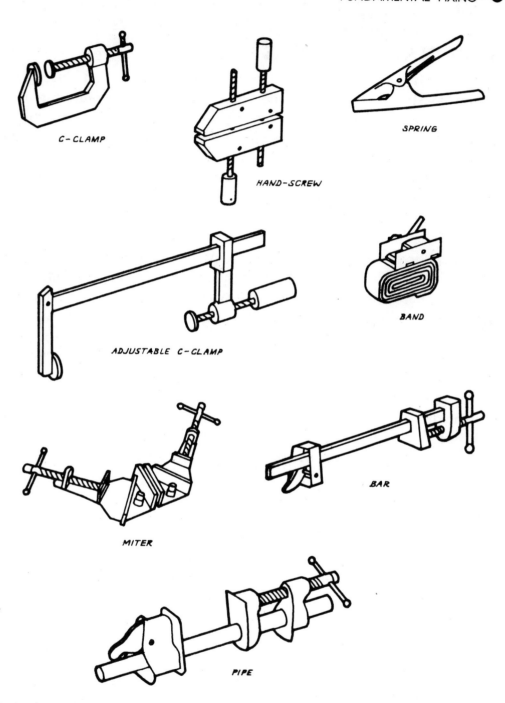

C-CLAMP

HAND-SCREW

SPRING

ADJUSTABLE C-CLAMP

BAND

MITER

BAR

PIPE

Basic clamps. No matter what kind or how many you have, it is never enough.

SOME CLAMPING SECRETS

Since glue is the essential repairing agent for furniture and since it must always have time to harden, the most important tools in any furniture repair kit are the clamps. No matter how many different kinds of clamps you own or can beg, borrow or steal, you do not have enough of the right kind. Even if you do have enough there are times when they will do you no good whatsoever and you will have to improvise some other way of holding two pieces of wood together.

You not only have to be creative about how you use your clamps, but you should also be aware of some dos and don'ts about clamping methods. The metal or wooden jaws of most clamps will damage the finish on your furniture. Professionals are always careful to place a piece of wood, cloth or cardboard between the clamp and the wood it is holding. An even better way of protecting your furniture is to glue a piece of felt, cardboard, rubber or even paper to each of the jaws on all of your clamps.

The pressure a clamp exerts against a joint should, as often as possible, be at right angles to the glue line. If the clamp is positioned off-center, there is a possibility that the pressure will be uneven and the joint will slip or become distorted. It is easy to say "keep your clamps at right angles to the glue line," but there are an amazing number of situations when that is impossible to do. Nevertheless, be aware of the dangers of slippage whenever you are setting clamps.

After the clamp is positioned you want to crank it down until the joint is so tight you can hardly see the glue line, right? Wrong. If the gluing surfaces fit accurately together and you have applied enough glue to all of those surfaces, all the clamp has to do is hold them firmly together so that they cannot move around. You want to tighten the clamp just until some of the excess glue has squeezed out of the glue line. Too much pressure will squeeze nearly all the glue out of a joint and there will not be enough to bond the wood. Too much pressure can also warp the wood you are gluing and sometimes cause your repair to break apart.

If you are using two or more clamps to hold a joint together, place the clamps against the repair so that the pressure they exert is evenly distributed all along the glue line. One way you can tell whether the clamps are equally tight is by observing the amount of glue that oozes out of the joint. If you have hardly any squeeze-out at one end of the joint and a lot at the other,

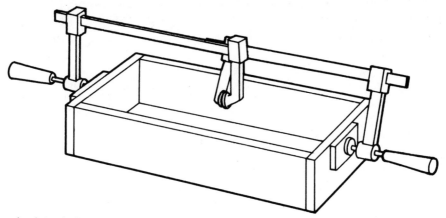

Sometimes a pair of short clamps can be utilized to do the work of a larger one.

you can assume one clamp is too loose and the other is too tight (or you did not apply enough glue).

Try to match the clamp to the job. Fragile rails, for example, do not require pipe clamps to hold them when a spring clamp will do as well. But if a pipe clamp is the only thing you have to work with, be extra careful about how much pressure you exert on the parts you are mending.

TWINE, TAPE AND TWISTS

When clamps cannot get a grip on odd-shaped pieces of wood, try cord, twine or masking tape. The best kind of cord to use is cotton clothesline,

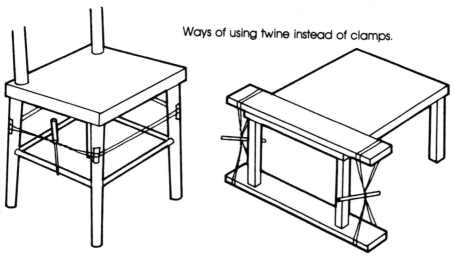

Ways of using twine instead of clamps.

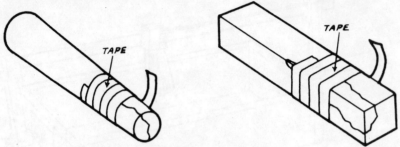

Ways of using masking tape in place of clamps.

since it is soft and strong, and does not scratch wood as much as other cords or twine. Like clamps, cord can chew into wood, so always put a pad of cloth or paper between it and the wood it touches.

If you are repairing say, the legs of a chair, there is no way you can tie a piece of clothesline tight enough to keep your joints together. What you can do is wrap the cord around the legs at least twice and tie it as tightly as possible, then push a screwdriver or a stick of wood between the strands and rotate it so that it twists the cord. When the cord is twisted tightly enough, jam your lever against a solid part of the chair (such as one of the leg rails) so that it cannot unwind.

The same principle of twisting cord to create proper pressure can be applied to larger furniture. Use boards to act as the jaws of your improvised clamp. Place a board on either side of the joint you are gluing and tie cord around both ends of the boards. Then twist both cords until the boards exert an equal pressure against the joint.

Masking tape is even better than cord if you are repairing small areas. It may leave some of its gum on the wood, but that can be cleaned off with turpentine or alcohol. Use it to bandage the corner of a tabletop, the split in a delicate rail or for any number of other small repairs.

MENDING CHAIRS, TABLES AND CASEWORK

If you are knowledgeable in preparing wood surfaces, if you understand the principles of gluing and have developed the knack of using clamps, you are fully prepared to handle practically any repair to the wooden parts of your furniture.

There are specific problems that you can expect to encounter with every type of furniture. Here are some of those problems and what to do about them.

Chairs

Chairs undergo more misuse, abuse, stress and strain than any other kind of furniture. They are pushed and pulled, tilted back on their legs, twisted and turned, and expected to withstand the abrupt shock of a couple hundred pounds of human flesh landing suddenly on their seats. Through all of this, chairs are supposed to look more or less delicate, which means that they are usually made up of delicate-looking parts.

The first thing you are likely to notice about a chair in need of restoration is that it wobbles when you sit in it. If you examine the chair closely you will probably discover one or more loose joints in the frame. If the joints will disassemble easily, pull them apart so you can tell which ones need regluing. Most chairs are made with mortise-and-tenon or dowel joints, which can be cleaned and reglued provided the sockets have not become enlarged. The sockets that are most susceptible to enlargement are the ones where the legs enter the bottom of a solid wooden seat; in upholstered or padded chairs they are where the legs intersect the seat frame at its corners. All loose joints should be corrected before you tackle any other repair.

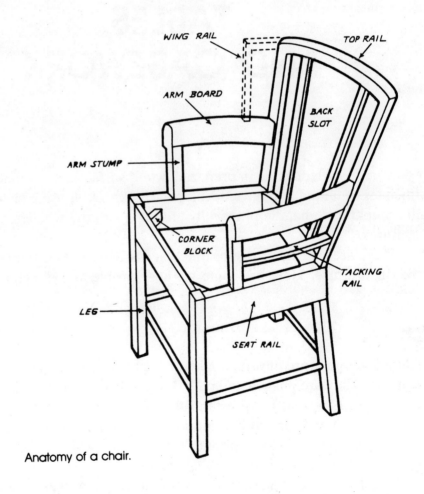

Anatomy of a chair.

TIGHTENING LOOSE JOINTS

The most reliable approach to an enlarged dowel socket is to drill or at least clean out the hole, and fill it with glue and a dowel. When the glue has dried, make the end of the dowel even with the wood around it and then redrill the socket. An alternative to doweling and redrilling the hole is to stuff the socket with wooden matches, toothpicks or wood chips. Small bits of wood will achieve the same joint sturdiness for a time, at least until the fillers work loose.

The leg joints on any framed seat should have glue blocks behind them. If there are none, add them. You can increase the holding power of existing blocks by taking them off and regluing them. Use a slightly larger screw to fasten them back in place. If you are making new glue blocks, they should be a minimum of 1½″ thick by 3″ long and fit snugly against all of the surfaces in the corner. Drill a guide hole through each end of the block; make the hole the diameter of the screw shank, then put a smaller pilot hole partway into the frame. Glue and screw the block into place.

In situations where a mortise or dowel hole has become too large for the tenon or dowel that fits into it, you may be able to tighten the joint with a spline. Cut a kerf through the center of the tenon or dowel, that is, split it in half with your saw. Now assemble the joint and drive a wedge of wood into the kerf until the wood spreads enough to form a tight union.

The arms in chairs are often doweled in place. They are just as frequently attached with hidden screws. To repair a loose arm, examine the area around the joint between the arm and back, looking for screw heads. Unlike dowels, which can be hidden between two pieces of wood, a screw must enter from an outer surface. Its head can then be covered by a wooden plug hammered into its countersink hole. The plugs can usually be pried loose with a knife or screwdriver blade. Once the screws are removed, a solid rap on the arm with your mallet should break the joint open. As always, any repair to the joint should include cleaning the wood, scraping away old glue and making certain that all dowels or screws fit securely into their holes (see Chapter 3).

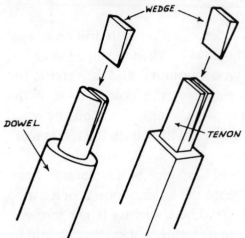

Cut a kerf in the center of a dowel or tenon and place it in its socket, then hammer a wedge into the slot.

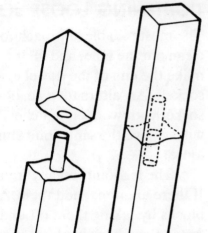

Broken members can often be mended with glue alone, but a dowel inserted into the break will strengthen it.

BROKEN PARTS

Surprisingly, almost any chair part (or other furniture part) that breaks can be successfully glued together again, particularly if the split is along the grain line. Clean the wood on both sides of the break and, if possible, insert dowels across the split before you glue the pieces together. You can pretty well assume that if a member has split or broken, it has also loosened any joint it is a part of; so when repairing the member, also clean out the end joints and reglue them.

The same repairs can be made if the break is across the grain, except that it is almost mandatory that you insert a dowel into the break before you glue it.

Tables

Fundamentally, every table is a wide, flat surface supported by legs. The legs may be fastened directly to the top or to a frame known as an apron, which in turn supports the tabletop. Most tables are constructed with metal dowel or mortise-and-tenon joints as well as a variety of hardware to support and strengthen the legs. Be very cautious when you are taking apart the joints in any table. There are often hidden wedges or splines in the joining parts which help to reinforce the joints; these can be troublesome to disassemble.

Once the joints holding the legs in place are opened, they can be repaired in the same manner as any chair or sofa leg. Wedges can be used to spread a tenon that is too small for its mortise; dowels can be replaced, repaired or reglued; splits and breaks in the wooden members can be doweled and glued (see Chapter 3).

Some tables are supported by pedestals which may have three or four legs joined to their base. If the legs are doweled to the pedestal and they loosen or break off, repair them as you would any dowel joint. The legs might also be attached to the pedestal with a mortise and tenon which may break. You can often repair the tenon by cutting it off and then inserting dowels in its place. You can also rout out part of the leg behind the tenon and shape a loose tenon which interlocks into the mortise on one side, and also fits into a dovetail rout chiseled out of the end of the leg.

Still other pedestals are hollow bases fitted over feet which are mortised together at right angles. There is usually a long bolt which extends from the tabletop down the center of the base and through the legs. If the pedestal develops a wobble, the feet have probably worn their mortises until they are no longer tight. Unbolt the pedestal and disassemble the feet from each other; hammer glue-coated shims into the sides of the loose tenon to tighten the mortise joint, then replace the pedestal.

THE TROUBLE WITH TABLETOPS

Tabletops warp. No matter how well they are constructed or supported, years of daily changes in the weather as well as constant use will distort them, particularly if they were finished on only one side. If the top of a table is finished, the finish material protects the wood from absorbing humidity, so moisture creeps in and out of the uncovered underside. If your table is warped during part of the year but corrects itself during the next season, wait until the warp disappears, then varnish all of the unfinished surfaces. Chances are the wood will stay put during the next weather change.

If a tabletop (or any large board) is permanently warped, the only lasting way you can correct it is to brace the underside with metal or wooden

Anatomy of a table.

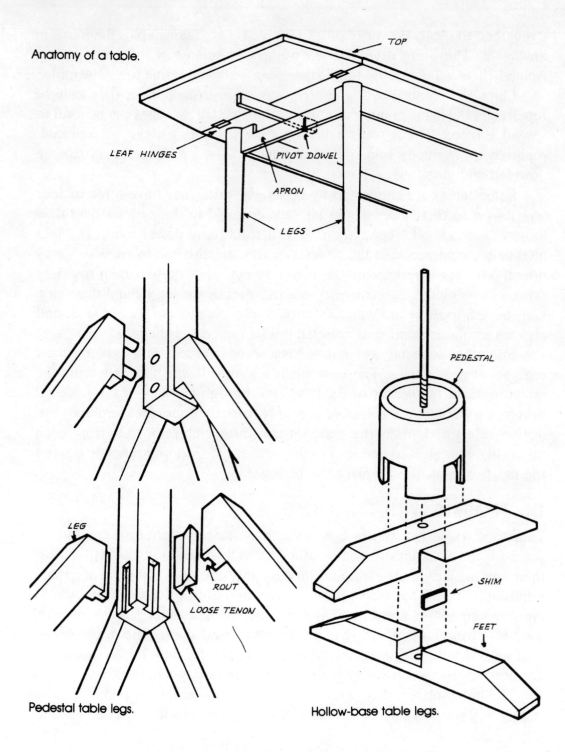

TOP

LEAF HINGES

PIVOT DOWEL

APRON

LEGS

PEDESTAL

LEG

ROUT

LOOSE TENON

SHIM

FEET

Pedestal table legs.

Hollow-base table legs.

cleats after you have straightened it. If the top curves down only slightly toward its unfinished side, wet the raw wood with a damp sponge and then clamp it by placing a pair of 2×4s on either side of the board and holding them together with C-clamps at each end. Then clamp pairs of 2×4s every 10″ along the length of the board and leave them in place for at least 24 hours.

Warping is caused by heat and moisture working on unsupported parts of the wood, but heat and moisture can also correct the warp in wood. If you are straightening a tabletop that is to be completely refinished, remove the finish so that you are working with the raw wood. Wrap the tabletop in rags, towels, paper or any other material that can be kept damp for several days, and then thoroughly soak it. Keep the material damp for four or five days so that the wood fibers become pliable enough to be clamped without splitting. Then remove the wet covering and clamp the tabletop every 10″ along its length. Each clamp should consist of two 2×4s that are long enough to extend beyond the tabletop. These are placed opposite each other on either side of the wood. The ends of the 2×4s are held tightly together with either ¼″ bolts or large C-clamps. When you have set all of the clamps in position, tighten them alternately until the pressure they exert is evenly distributed across the wood and the tabletop is flat. Place the assembly in a warm, dry place for several days. But don't forget it—the wood may have a tendency to split as it dries out. To keep it from shrinking and cracking, loosen and then immediately retighten the bolts or C-clamps several times a day. When the wood is completely dry, it should be flat. If it is not, dampen and clamp it again.

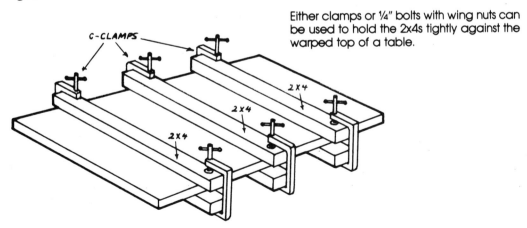

Either clamps or ¼″ bolts with wing nuts can be used to hold the 2x4s tightly against the warped top of a table.

C-CLAMPS

2X4

2X4

2X4

Cleats must be placed across the wood grain as soon as the tabletop is removed from its clamps.

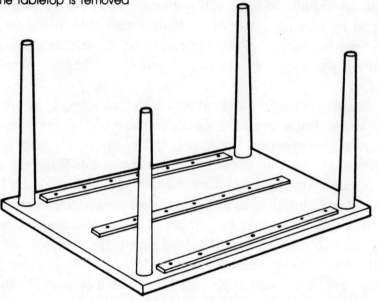

As soon as the clamps are removed, glue-screw cleats to the underside of the board, positioning each cleat so that it runs *across* the grain of the wood. The cleats should be prepared in advance with pilot holes drilled and screws driven almost through the holes.

You do not want the warped wood to be without some kind of support for any longer than is absolutely necessary, nor should it be left unprotected. So refinish both of its sides immediately to keep moisture from getting at it.

MENDING SPLITS

When a tabletop isn't warping it may decide to split, or the glue between its boards may dry out so that a joint or two comes apart. If the split runs with the grain of the wood, pry it open with a screwdriver or chisel just enough to get a good coating of glue into the break. Then clamp the wood together with bar clamps until the glue dries.

If the split is so ragged that regluing it is impossible, you will probably have to cut away the damaged surfaces with a saw or chisel and insert a wood patch. The difficulty here is to find a wood that is compatible with the tabletop, and cut it so that its grain goes in the same direction as the grain that surrounds it. The patch should be glued in place and refinished to match the rest of the top as closely as possible.

Completely broken boards or open seams between planks can be cleaned of their old glue and reglued. Always consider, too, replacing worn or broken dowels, or inserting new dowels every 6″ to 8″ along the joint if none were used originally.

There is another way of holding two boards together in a butt joint: using butterfly patches. The butterfly patch is an hourglass-shaped piece of wood that should be no more than half the thickness of the wood you are joining. You can cut butterfly patches from any material, although hardwood is preferable. The design of the patch should incorporate flared ends, which can be at almost any angle. When you have cut the butterflies, clamp the split pieces together and trace the outline of the patches on the underside of the boards. Then rout out a bed for each patch, making it slightly shallower than the butterfly is thick. The bed should be as snug a fit as you can get. Now glue the patches in their mortises and clamp them in place. When the glue dries, sand the patches flush with the surface around them and protect them with an appropriate finishing material.

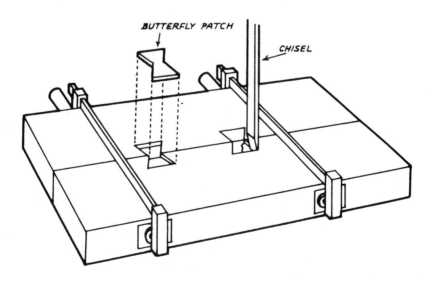

Hold the split boards together with clamps until you have cut the butterfly beds. Glue the butterfly patch in place and clamp it until the glue has dried.

DROP LEAFS

Drop-leaf tables are vulnerable to wear at their hinges as well as at the braces that support the leaves. The hinges are repaired in the same manner as any hinge (see Chapter 3), and usually do not require any disassembly of the table frame itself.

TABLE SUPPORTS

Table leaves are supported by a pivot, gate leg or hinged brace, and all three can become loose or even break. The pivot support is a piece of wood that rotates out of the table apron. It is held in place by a dowel inserted through its center and into sockets drilled into the underside of the table and the table apron. If the pivot dowel breaks or becomes loose, the top must be taken off its apron and the support lifted out of its position. The dowel sockets can be filled and redrilled and the dowel, of course, can also be replaced. If the pivot support is broken or badly worn, use it as a pattern to shape a new one from a straight-grained hardwood such as oak.

Hinged supports sometimes break and can be replaced with new wooden parts, but more often they develop hinge troubles. A metal hinge pin can wear down or enlarge the hole in its barrel, causing a loose hinge and therefore a wobbly joint. If you cannot find a hinge pin big enough to fit tightly in the hinge, you will have to replace the entire hinge.

Gate-leg supports may be attached to the table frame with hinges or dowels. If the hinges work loose or become worn, they are repaired or replaced like any hinge (see Chapter 3). But before you worry about the hinges, check the gate leg and the table itself for any loose joints or broken members and repair them first. This may entail disassembling all or part of the table so that the joints can be properly cleaned and reglued.

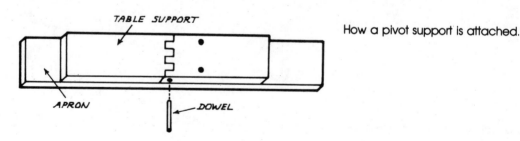

How a pivot support is attached.

TABLE SUPPORT

APRON

DOWEL

Some gate legs are held between the bottom of the apron and the top of the leg rail with pivot dowels. These can enlarge their sockets, causing the gate to develop a case of the ricketys. If you have to disassemble the apron and frame to reglue loose joints, you can repair the gate pivots at the same time without any particular difficulty. But if only the pivots are dysfunctional, you have a problem.

Turn the table upside down and look at the bottom of the leg rail under the gate. If you are lucky, the pivot (or top) dowel extends through the bottom of the rail, and you can drill or perhaps even pry it out of its socket. If this dowel does not extend through the rail, slide a saw blade between the bottom of the gate and the top of the leg rail, and cut the dowel. The gate can then be pulled down out of its socket in the apron. Fill the apron socket with a new dowel and redrill it, and/or replace the worn dowel with a slightly larger dowel.

Proceed to the bottom dowel in the gate; this is treated differently. Clean out the dowel socket in the gate so that it is slightly larger than the dowel you will be using. Now drill all the way through the existing dowel hole in the leg rail, cut a kerf in one end of the dowel, and cut the dowel long enough to enter the gate socket and reach through to the bottom of the leg rail. Insert the pivot dowel in the rail and glue it, then put the gate in place and insert the bottom dowel through the underside of the leg rail. You can use glue in the hole in the rail, but hammer a wedge into the kerf at the bottom of the dowel to make it absolutely tight.

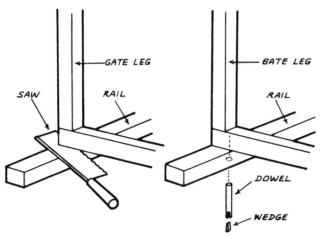

The pivot at the bottom of a gate hinge may have to be sawed in half. When replacing the pivot, put a wedge in the end of the dowel to make sure the dowel fits tightly in its hole.

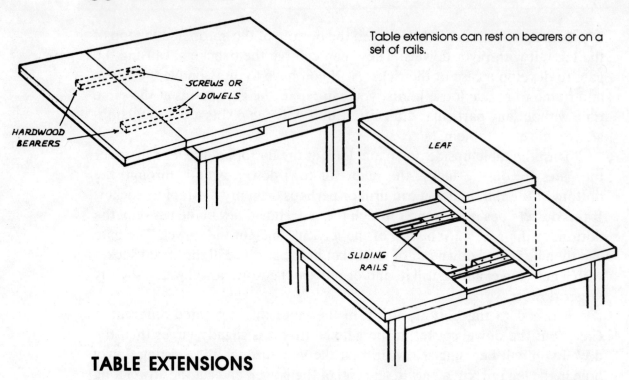

Table extensions can rest on bearers or on a set of rails.

TABLE EXTENSIONS

There are two kinds of extension tables. One type has a set of interlocking rails screwed to the underside of the top, allowing the top to be pulled apart and leaves inserted. The other type has a top that lifts slightly to allow its leaves to be pulled out from above the apron. The top then drops down into place. When the leaves are in use they are supported by wooden bearers that either are hinged to the apron or slide out from under the top through notches in the apron.

The wooden bearers can warp or split and must be replaced. Use the old bearers as a pattern and cut new ones from oak or any other straight-grained hardwood. If either a bearer or the notch it slides through is worn down, it can be built up to its proper thickness by gluing shims to the worn edges.

Extension rails are bulky, so are awkward to repair. Should they become really worn or split (which is rare), it is easiest to buy a new rail assembly at almost any building supply store. The rails are held to the underside of the tabletop with long screws, but rarely glue, so their replacement is normally not difficult. The screws should be checked occasionally for looseness; they should be kept tight.

Casework

Casework is a box in all its forms. Often a chest, bureau, desk, cabinet or bookcase will incorporate drawers and/or doors and very often will have some short, stubby form of legs. The essence of any casework is its rigidity, which in turn relies on tight joints that are most often reinforced by glue blocks. Don't ever hesitate to add a glue block or some kind of brace when repairing a glue joint. They can never lessen the stability of the furniture and usually they will help.

BACKS

When casework becomes shaky, the first place to look is its back. Backs have two functions: to keep the piece square and to give it rigidity. Antiques usually have backs made of solid wood, either a complete panel or a series of boards that have been joined together. Because they are solid wood, backs can warp or split. As soon as either occurs or if the panel simply comes loose, the entire structure will begin to shift out of alignment, causing such headaches as doors and drawers that stick or refuse to work altogether, and joints that begin to work loose.

Backs are usually fitted into rabbets cut out of the inner edges of the top, bottom and sides of a cabinet and are held there with screws or small nails. Although the back panel may be any thickness, ¼" stock is usually used. If the original wood has split or warped it can be repaired either by clamping it or gluing its pieces together. However, consider replacing the back altogether with either plywood or hardboard, both of which swell and shrink considerably less than any piece of solid wood.

Even before you repair or replace the back of your casework, ferret out the other problems in the piece—loose joints, broken members or what have you. It is always easier to make repairs to casework if the back, hardware, loose shelving, drawers and doors are first removed. Loose joints should be opened, cleaned and reglued. Broken members must be reglued and, whenever possible, strengthened with dowels. Details on these repairs are found in Chapter 3.

TOPS

If the top of some casework is in need of restoration, your first problem is likely to be disengaging it from the sides of the unit. Look underneath it for any signs of screws and/or glue blocks. If you don't find any, figure that the top has been doweled in place. In either case, once all obvious fasteners have been removed, you can gently tap the underside of the top with your mallet until it comes free. If the top is split or warped, repair it as you would a tabletop or any large board (see pages 59, 61–62), using clamps, butterfly patches, dowels or anything else the repair calls for.

LEGS

The legs attached to the bottom of casework can take many forms and are normally well secured to the frame of the piece. Should they come loose, the repair will be quite obvious and most often will amount to regluing and doweling broken joints or members.

The legs of furniture are often bored to accept casters, which in turn take an awesome amount of stress that can break off a piece of the leg. To repair a split or broken leg:

1. Assemble the pieces and hold them together with masking tape wrapped tightly around the wood.

2. Drill out the socket that holds the caster and fit the hole with a dowel.

3. Disassemble the pieces and glue them, then hold them together with a clamp or clamps until the glue has hardened.

4. When the glue is dry you can allow the bottom of the leg to remain as is; you can hammer a glide into the dowel; or you can drill into the dowel and fit the caster back in the leg.

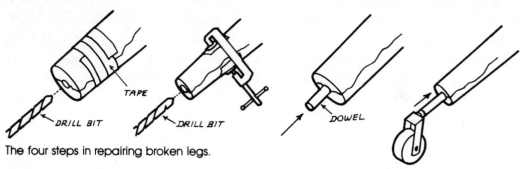

The four steps in repairing broken legs.

CABINET DOORS

The doors on cabinets can split, warp, chip and get out of line. If they are warped, dampen the wood and clamp it for 24 hours. Splits can be reglued. Look at the hinges very carefully with any door that does not open or close properly. Often the hinges can be remortised or repositioned, their screws can be replaced or the hinges can be shimmed to make a slightly warped door work (see Chapter 3). The easiest way to repair the loose joints in a cabinet door is to screw L-shaped corner plates into the back of the joint; the most durable way is to dismantle the joints, clean off the old glue and reglue them. When you are clamping a door after gluing, be careful to set it so that it is absolutely square as the glue dries.

Small cabinet doors that have warped can sometimes be straightened by dampening the wood and attaching a cable and turnbuckle diagonally across the back of the door. Tighten the turnbuckle until the door straightens, and leave it there when you hang the door back on its frame.

A warped door can also be made to fit properly in its frame by planing down all or part of its edges. Planes incorporate a beveled blade which is essentially a chisel. It follows, then, that a chisel can be used in the same manner as a plane, although it is usually employed in smaller areas. If you hold a chisel with the beveled side of the blade flat against the wood, you can produce fine shavings by pushing the tool forward with one hand while holding the blade down firmly by pressing the fingers of your other hand against the blade near the cutting edge. If you shave wood with the beveled side of the blade up, you will remove more material with each stroke, but it is more difficult to control how much wood you take off. In either case, keep your finger against the cutting blade.

Sliding doors can swell or their tracks can shrink, making them stick. If the tracks swell and become too large for the door, you can fill their sides by gluing shims inside the grooves. Doors that are too large to slide properly in their tracks can be planed down along their top and bottom edges, but taper them only enough to move freely in their tracks again.

DRAWERS

The most common drawer malady is that they stick. This can occur because the drawer is overloaded or because part of its contents have gotten caught between the unit and its frame. When you simply cannot make the drawer open, try getting at it by removing the drawers above and below it or, as a last resort, taking off the back of the casework.

But drawers can also stick because the wood has swollen or the drawer runners have become rough. If they are really rough, sand them lightly and then give them a coating of hard wax or soap. Otherwise just coat them with the soap or wax. The runners or one of the joints in the drawer itself may have worked loose, in which case they should be reglued. Usually this requires disassembly of the drawer.

Drawers in good furniture are usually assembled with dovetail joints, which are a series of small, interlocking flared tenons that can be broken off if you mindlessly whack away at them with a mallet. If you cannot work the joint apart by pulling it with your hands, place a block of wood inside the corner and tap your hammer against it so that pressure will be evenly distributed the full length of the joint.

A common problem with drawers is that their bottoms split or shrink and even fall out of the grooves that hold them between the sides. You could go to the trouble of straightening a warped drawer bottom or regluing pieces of it that have split. But modern cabinetmakers nearly always use ¼" hardboard for their drawer bottoms, primarily because it is strong and will

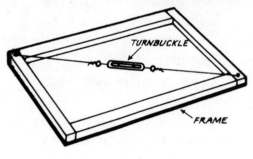

By attaching a wire diagonally across the back of a warped door and tightening it with a turnbuckle, you can sometimes straighten the misalignment. The wire and turnbuckle must remain in place.

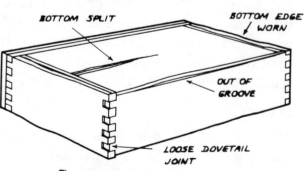

The areas of a drawer that can cause problems.

not react to changes in the weather. It is usually easier, and often better for the drawer, if you replace an imperfect bottom with a new piece of hardboard or plywood. If the bottom is fitted into grooves dadoed out of the sides of the drawer and you are using hardboard or plywood, you can glue the bottom if you wish. Any other material that you select should not be glued in the slots—it needs room to expand and shrink without splitting.

The frame that holds a drawer can also come apart at its joints, or its members can split or break. These can all be replaced or glued back together again, but be sure that the drawer runners are positioned in exactly the same places they were originally, or the drawers may not work properly when you are done.

Veneer

Veneer is usually between ¼₂″ and ¹⁄₆₄″ thick and is liable to be made of any of 25,000 woods, which makes it hard to identify. First the ancient Egyptians, then the Greeks, Romans, Chinese and finally modern furniture makers have pasted paper-thin sheets of expensive decorative woods to the fronts, sides and tops of furniture made with some cheaper, less attractive local lumber. Veneer isn't cheating—it is an old, old form of furniture decoration.

Veneer is extremely thin, and therefore very fragile. And given enough time and humidity changes, almost any glue holding the veneer will eventually dry out and lose its sticking power. At that point you will find edges that lift away from corners or blisters in the middle of the veneer. Neither of these may appear to be critical but they almost always lead to far worse damage—for example, liquid spilled on the veneer could seep between it and the core wood and cause major blistering. Or someone might catch the loose corner of a veneered top with a sleeve and wind up tearing half the top apart.

LOOSE EDGES

A loose edge poses one problem: how to get the glue spread between the veneer and its core. It is not easy to do, but carefully pry the veneer away from the core with the blade of a spatula or dull knife, and try to scrape off as much of the old glue in the split as you can. Then inject some cream or white glue between the core and veneer with a glue injector. If you have no injector available, squirt the glue in directly from its bottle and spread it around as best you can with a knife blade. Then clamp or weight the repair for at least 24 hours, or hold the edge down with masking tape. Be sure to wipe off all glue that seeps out of the repair as quickly as possible with a rag dipped in warm water.

BLISTERS

You have some alternatives with blisters. Blisters occur when there is little or no glue under the veneer, or moisture has swelled the core wood so that it bubbles up. If you have a notion that there still may be some glue under the blister, you might iron it out. Place a sheet of aluminum foil over the blister and rub it along the grain with a moderately warm iron. If you are able to iron the wood flat, clamp it for a few hours. If the blister bubbles up again, there is probably not enough glue under the veneer. Slit the veneer along the grain on both sides of the blister with a craft knife and inject white or cream glue under the veneer, then clamp or weight the blister for at least 12 hours. If the blister rises after you are finished, go back to the warm iron and aluminum foil. At least now you know there is glue under the blister.

Surface Repairs

Before you sand the surfaces of your furniture, there may be gouges, scratches, dents or minor splits in the wood that must be evened off or filled. At this point you must bring the entire surface of the wood to the same plane either by removing some of the surface or filling it in.

Gouges and dents can sometimes be raised, whether the surface is solid or a veneer, by placing a damp cloth over the depression and ironing it with a warm iron. If the ironing process fails, you can fill the mar the same way you would a scratch, cut, gouge or open seam.

The art of hiding a defect in wood surfaces requires meticulousness and an eye for color, which you either have or don't have. It also requires patience, which can be learned. The materials used to fill minor depressions can be wood dough, plastic wood filler or shellac sticks, but the odds of your procuring any of these in the exact color to match the wood you are repairing are something like a million to one. So you have to mix your fillers and apply them to the wood, then mix them again, adding lighteners or darkeners until you achieve a color that, if it is not exactly right, will at least be not too noticeable. If the wood you are repairing has any really dark streaks in it and the repair runs with the grain, you may be able to get away with just a streak of iodine applied with an India ink pen, which no one but you will notice.

SHELLAC STICKS

The most successful crack fillers are the shellac sticks, which can be purchased in a full range of colors. They come as hard bars of solid shellac which you heat directly or rub against the heated blade of a narrow spatula. The heat melts the shellac so that you can then rub it into the defect. Mound it slightly above the surrounding surface of the wood; it will dry within minutes, but let it harden overnight. Then, using a chisel held absolutely vertical, scrape away the excess. Finally, sand the area with a superfine-grit abrasive.

WOOD FILLERS

The wood fillers sold today come in several forms and a variety of colors, allowing you to more or less match the color of the wood you are filling. If you need to match exactly the color of the wood you are filling, and you have a scrap piece of the wood on hand or can remove a piece from the frame without reducing its strength, you can make your own filler. Saw the piece of scrap and collect all of the sawdust. Pour a white glue (acetate) into a dish and mix the sawdust with it until it reaches the consistency of putty. Now fill the wood and allow the mixture to dry. When dry it should, in theory, be the same color and texture as the wood you are repairing.

Wood fillers are supposed to fill minor defects, that is, shallow digs or small holes, not large splits. They shouldn't be used in places that will subsequently be drilled to accept screws—fillers don't have the holding power a screw needs. Remember that all fillers contract as they dry. So when you apply them, mound the material above the surrounding wood; with luck, the filler will sink evenly into the hole and dry level, or nearly level, with the wood surface. More often, they will sink below the surface, at which point you apply more filler. When you are finished applying filler, you should have a small bump which can be sanded down flush with the wood. All wood fillers can be sanded, and all will accept either paint or a clear finish. However, unless the outline of the repair is as irregular as the grain and the filler is absolutely the proper color and shade of the wood, you can presume that the repair will be noticeable under a clear finish.

Always work with the grain when you are filling cracks in wood. Try to blend the filler into the surface with as many irregular edges as you can, so that the filler, whatever it may be, becomes a part of the wood pattern.

PATCHES

The problem with patching wood surfaces that are larger than the width of a crack or open seam is to find the wood you can use to make your patch. Sometimes there may be a piece of wood hidden somewhere inside or at the bottom of the furniture that can be replaced so that you can use it for patching. If you are patching veneer, veneer squares can be purchased at many woodworking supply stores and at lumberyards that specialize in hardwoods. Take a piece of the veneer with you when you go shopping so that you can get the closest possible match.

Assuming you are able to buy enough of the right wood to make your patch, the painstaking part of the repair is to fit the new wood as precisely into its bed as possible. Your primary aim when patching is not so much to repair the deep gouge or damaged area as it is to successfully hide all of the hard work you will go through.

Make your patches as irregular as possible, particularly when they are cutting across the grain lines. Always work with the grain; try to find a part of the grain in your patching material that more or less approximates the grain you are repairing.

Procedure for Patching Wood

The procedure for making a patch in wood is identical for solid wood and veneer. It begins by taping three sides of a piece of tracing paper over the damaged area and marking the irregular outline of your patch somewhere outside the borders of the damaged area. Design as irregular a patch as possible. Now slip a piece of veneer under the paper and adjust its grain until it is the least noticeable when it lines up beneath your outline. If possible, clamp the veneer in position; otherwise hold it firmly in place. Using a craft knife, cut around the outside of the patch lines, through the veneer as well as the old material.

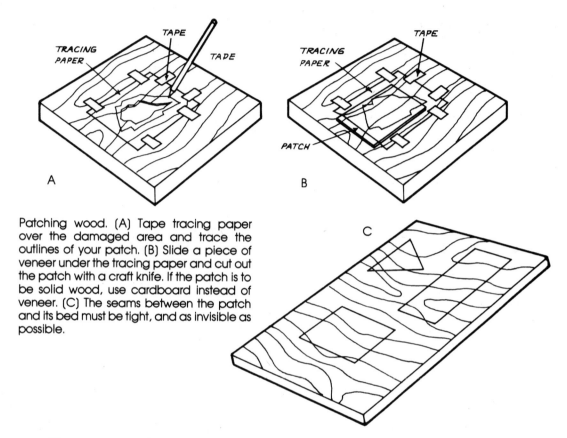

Patching wood. (A) Tape tracing paper over the damaged area and trace the outlines of your patch. (B) Slide a piece of veneer under the tracing paper and cut out the patch with a craft knife. If the patch is to be solid wood, use cardboard instead of veneer. (C) The seams between the patch and its bed must be tight, and as invisible as possible.

If you are cutting a patch for insertion into solid wood, use a piece of cardboard instead of veneer. The cardboard will become a template for cutting your patch piece; the craft knife will scratch the outline of the patch bed into the wood to be repaired.

If you are replacing veneer, once you have cut the patch you need only remove the tracing paper and dig out any excess veneer from its bed. With solid wood, position the cardboard template on your patch wood and cut out the wood. You must also dig out the bed with a chisel until it is deep enough for the exact dimensions of the patch. Sand the patch bed and apply a strong glue, then insert the patch and clamp it until the glue is dry. The entire area should be sanded smooth and refinished when your patch has dried in place. The seams between the patch and its bed should be tight. If they are not, fill them with wood putty and cover that with shellac before applying any finish to the repair.

5

FIXING
FURNITURE FINISHES

An old finish becomes dull and scratched, and the longer you stare at it, the surer you are that the only remedy is to go down to the raw wood and start over again. But there are no rules for determining whether a piece actually needs your extensive blood, sweat and tender care or not. To some, minor scratches and stains may be entirely acceptable while to others they demand removal. Actually, unless the finish is full of cracks and blisters and is extensively flaking off, whether or not you refinish it becomes a matter of personal taste.

Even if you are dead certain you want to remove the old finish, it pays to clean it with benzine first, if only to clearly define where the problems exist. Simply soak a clean, soft cloth in the benzine and rub the surface. Keep changing cloths, soaking them with benzine and rubbing the finish until it is absolutely clean; then wipe it dry. You may be surprised at how good the condition of the finish really is. If you decide it does not need to be removed after all, apply a good-quality cleanser-conditioner and then a furniture polish. The cleanser-conditioner helps to bring out the grain and color of the wood, and hides any minor scratches. It also protects wood against both heat and dryness.

How to Determine an Old Finish

If you decide to remove the old finish, it helps to know just what it is so that you can use the proper finish removers.

Other than paint, which is obvious, furniture may have been covered with shellac, varnish or lacquer, which are difficult to tell apart without specifically testing for them. The test involves putting one drop of denatured alcohol and a drop of lacquer thinner on an inconspicuous corner of the finish. What happens to different finishes when you apply a drop of alcohol or lacquer thinner is this:

	Shellac (Solvent: Alcohol)	Varnish (Solvent: Turpentine)	Lacquer (Solvent: Lacquer Thinner)
1–2 drops denatured alcohol	Dissolves	Not affected	Not affected
1–2 drops lacquer thinner	Not affected	Blisters	Smears

Adding a New Topcoat

You may find that all you really need to do is apply a new topcoat over the old finish. Don't mix finishes—if the piece is varnished, varnish it; if it is lacquered, use lacquer. You can apply a new coat of any of the clear finishes provided you abrade all the sheen on the old coat so that the new material has something it can adhere to. Sand the old finish with a superfine-grit abrasive or a #4/0 steel wool. Rub with the grain of the wood until there is no gloss left; then wipe clean with a tack rag and apply your new topcoat.

The Magic of Glaze

Still another way of putting new life into an old finish is to sand it lightly to remove the sheen, and then apply a thin coating of glaze, which will help to bring out the wood color and also hide minor blemishes. You can buy glaze, or you can dilute almost any stain to a 50-50 mixture with gum turpentine. The color of stain you use need not be exactly the color of the old finish, but it should be reasonably close. Wipe the glaze over the finish. If you don't like the looks of it, wipe it off again with a rag dipped in turpentine. When you have achieved the results you want, allow the glaze to dry for at least 24 hours; then seal the surface with a coat of one part shellac mixed with eight parts alcohol, followed by a topcoat of whatever clear finish you are using.

Getting Rid of Stains

There are all kinds of surprising tricks for getting stains out of furniture woods. Here are a few of them.

Water. Water stains on furniture finish can be removed with either of two methods. Lay a thick blotter over the spot and press it with a warm iron until the spot disappears. If that doesn't work, try dipping a pad of fine #4/0 steel wool in a good furniture polish or liquid wax and rub the spot gently.

Milk and alcohol. Milk, or any liquid containing milk or cream, should never be left on any finish for very long because milk acts as a mild paint remover. Wipe up spilled milk immediately, and treat the spot in either of the two ways recommended for removing alcohol stains: 1) Rub the spot with a damp cloth dipped in ammonia. When the stain is gone, polish the area with lemon oil.

2) Rub the stain with your finger dipped in a wax paste, silver polish, linseed oil, or wet cigar or cigarette ashes.

Candle wax. Freeze the wax by holding an ice cube against it. Then crumble it off the wood with your fingers or a dull kitchen knife. Rub the area with a cloth dipped in liquid furniture wax and wipe the finish dry. Keep rubbing with the wax and drying the area until all of the candle wax has disappeared.

White spots. Who knows where white spots keep cropping up from? Unless you know they are from milk, rub them with a cloth dipped in motor oil, vegetable shortening, lard, salad oil or wax *and* cigarette or cigar ashes. What kind of oil you use is not as important as mixing it with the ashes. Rub the area until the spot disappears, and wipe the surface with a dry cloth.

Scratches

If a scratch is in the finish but does not penetrate the wood beneath it, clean the area thoroughly and test the finish with a drop of alcohol and another drop of lacquer thinner. Apply the appropriate solvent for the finish with a small artist's brush. Paint the solvent diagonally across the scratch, feathering out along the edges so that the finish can dissolve and blend into it. Let the area dry completely, then rub it with a dry cloth and buff with wax.

feathering out along the edges so that the finish can dissolve and blend into it. Let the area dry completely, then rub it with a dry cloth and buff with wax.

A scratch that digs into the wood can often be filled with wax or a shellac stick that is melted into the cut. But you may find it is easier to blend in the proper color if you use an oil stain or artist's acrylic paints. Clean the damaged area with benzine and then fill the scratch with your stain. Allow the repair to dry completely, then rub it with the appropriate shellac stick or pigment solvent to blend in the stain.

If the scratch is really deep, you can build it up until it is flush with the surface by filling it with several coats of diluted finish material. Give each coat a chance to dry before covering it again, and try to put it only in the scratch. When the mar is filled, clean the entire surface and apply a new topcoat, which will not only protect your repair, but help to blend it as well.

Tricks with Chemical Removers

If you decide to remove a finish, you could be old-fashioned about it and sand it off. But too much sanding can be hazardous to the surface of the wood and is not particularly efficient either. At any rate it is not as efficient as using a chemical stripper. On the negative side, chemical strippers can be hazardous to your health.

The three kinds of strippers available are oil based, water based and water rinsed. Then there is lye. Lye is quick, thorough and will take your skin off as easily as it will any finish material. It has to be watched closely because it will also dismantle all the glue joints in your furniture, which is why it is seldom recommended for use on furniture. It is good for doing balustrades, door and window molding and even old shutters, but these have few if any glued joints; and the wood must always be sanded afterwards.

For the record, you can make a lye bathtub out of plywood panels and then line it with plastic sheeting, which is one of the few things going that is impervious to lye. Fill your tub with lye mixed with water, and soak whatever it is you are stripping in the solution. As soon as the finish has lifted from the wood sufficiently to be scrubbed off with steel wool or a wire brush, remove the piece and flush it thoroughly with water. Then scrub off the remaining finish with a scraper or steel wool. The wood will be "furry" after it has dried, and require a light sanding.

The chemical strippers are somewhat less caustic than lye, but still should not be handled with your bare hands. Rubber gloves are much more durable than plastic ones. You will need a good supply of rags and newspapers; old paintbrushes that you can afford to throw away after you are through working; some coffee cans; a variety of putty knives and paint scrapers; steel wool; an ice pick or awl; old toothbrushes; and perhaps an old-fashioned beer-can opener. The assortment of small, pointed objects is for digging out stubborn pieces of finish in the cracks and curves of the molding and millwork.

Whatever chemical stripper you use (they all do a pretty decent job), follow the manufacturer's instructions, which always begin with the suggestion that you work in a well-ventilated room so that toxic and flammable vapors cannot build up around you.

There are compound and paste forms of the strippers sold at most paint and hardware stores. They are meant to adhere to vertical surfaces and evaporate more slowly than the liquids, which is why some people prefer them even if they are working on a horizontal surface. In any case, the procedure for using a chemical stripper is approximately the same no matter what product you select.

ABCs OF STRIPPING

Pour some of the stripper in a coffee can and paint a thick coating on the finish using an old brush. Brush once, or even pat the stripper on the wood, but do not brush it out. The moment the stripper touches a surface it begins to form a skin that helps the chemical act on the finish rather than dissipate in the air. Wait about 15 or 20 minutes; when you see the finish material bubbling, blistering and wrinkling, it is ready to be scraped off. You can use a paint scraper, a putty knife, a wire brush or any impromptu scraper to get the sludge off the wood. When the bulk of it is scraped off, sand what is left with #2/0 steel wool pads. Remember that for the moment, the stripper has also softened the wood, making it particularly vulnerable to gouging by the sharp edges of whatever scraping tool you are wielding. So work carefully. The ice pick, toothbrush and can opener are useful for getting into tiny corners and around curved surfaces.

Unless there are only one or two coats of finish on the wood, you will most likely need more than one application of stripper before the piece is completely clean. The usual recommendation is that you strip a relatively small area, then go on to the next small area and so on, until you have done the entire piece once. Then go back and go over the spots that still have finish on them, using fresh stripper and clean tools. The recommendation works, but professional paint strippers, who charge their customers for the chemicals and don't worry about how much they buy, have a different technique. The professionals literally flood a large area, wait for it to blister and then begin stripping. As the parts they have not reached begin to dry, they soak them again, constantly keeping them buried under chemicals until they have a chance to scrape them. By the time a professional gets to the end of the job, the last areas have been soaked so often that scraping them becomes almost academic. The pros use a lot more stripper than most people, but they can also clean seven or eight layers of century-old paint off 100 square feet of intricate molding in a day.

PREPARING WOOD

You cannot strip a piece of furniture with a chemical stripper and then slap on a new finish. The chemical strippers all leave a residue of chemicals and wax on the wood. This must be removed, or it will go right to work on the new finish and strip that too.

The best neutralizing-cleaning agent to use on wood that has been stripped with a chemical is gum turpentine. Apply it to the wood with some #2/0 steel wool and wash down every inch of surface. Let the turpentine soak into the wood for a few minutes, then wipe it off and allow the piece to dry overnight.

When the wood is dry, you may find a shadow of the old finish color still clinging to the surface. The hue can often enhance the look of the new finish you apply, so you could leave it. Or you can sand it off using a superfine-grit abrasive.

Finishing Supplies

No matter what finish you apply to furniture, there are a few staples that you should keep on hand. They are:

Alcohol. This is both a thinner and solvent for shellac. It also strips shellac better than a chemical stripper.

Linseed oil. You will need this to mix with some paints and stains.

Turpentine. The primary solvent for most paints, enamels and varnishes, including the urethanes.

Benzine. A first-rate general-purpose solvent.

Mineral spirits. An alternative to turpentine, used as both a thinner and solvent.

Waxes. There are many kinds, but all of them consist of beeswax, paraffin carnauba wax and turpentine, and help any finish resist moisture.

Pumice. A powder made from ground up lava, used to rub down the final coats of a finish. It comes in several grades; for furniture, use FF and FFF.

Rottenstone. Shale ground into a finer powder than pumice. It will produce a smoother finish than pumice.

Tack rags. If you don't buy them, you can make your own by dipping a lint-free rag in a solution of three parts varnish and one part turpentine.

The Finishing Process

All kinds of stages can be gone through when applying a finish to your furniture, but not all the basic steps described here are required on every project.

BLEACHING

You can bleach water marks, ink and other stains in raw wood with ordinary household bleach. You can also lighten a dark board to make its color conform to the other woods in the furniture, or take the natural color out of any wood if you want to have a light or honey-colored finish.

Heat the wood you are bleaching with a spotlight or by putting it in the sunlight. Then soak it in undiluted household bleach (or ammonia). Keep the wood wet until it has lost its discoloration—you may have to apply the bleach several times. When you have achieved the lightness you want, wash off the bleach with a solution of 50% water and 50% white vinegar, then wipe it dry. The wood should dry further for at least 12 hours at over 70°F before you sand it lightly with a fine- or superfine-grit abrasive.

Be aware that all that liquid can "cup" the wood, that is, bend its edges upward. As a precaution, as you wash off the bleach also dampen the underside of the wood to equalize the moisture content in the wood.

PRESTAINING

The reverse of bleaching is done when you have a variably colored wood such as walnut or teak which you want to have a constant dark color. You can achieve a uniform shade by brushing the light areas with a water-base stain. The water-base stains are inexpensive powders that are mixed with water. They dry quickly and can be darkened simply by applying more stain. However, the water content will swell the wood fibers and raise the grain so that the wood will have to be sanded afterward. When you have applied enough coats to get the coloration you want, allow the stain to dry thoroughly before you proceed to the next finishing stage.

STAINING

Stains, unlike paint or varnish, are made to soak into the fibers of the wood. There are numerous penetrating resin stains sold on the market. They all dry dust free and will not run, sag or show brush marks. You can either pour the stain on the wood and then spread it with a brush, or rub it into the wood with a cloth. In either case, the stain will protect the surface by solidifying chemicals within the fibers of the wood. Always apply it with the grain so that it can get in between the fibers. The commercially mixed stains usually come out lighter than you expect them to, which requires that you either apply more coats, mix together various colors or add artist's colors to them. There is an alternative to buying a ready-made stain, and that is to make your own.

Buy a can of clear penetrating stain oil, at least one tube of artist's burnt umber and one tube of burnt sienna. Together, sienna and umber will produce just about any shade of brown when they are mixed into the penetrating oil; you can also add any other artist's colors you wish. It pays to test any stain you have concocted on a hidden corner of the furniture to make sure you are getting the color you want. Also allow for the fact that stain continues to darken wood until it has dried. The color can be arrested at any time by wiping the surface of the wood with a clean cloth. It can also be lightened if you wash the wood with turpentine before (and sometimes after) the stain has dried completely.

You can play tricks with stains to make some parts of your furniture lighter or darker. It is possible to create a framing effect, for example, by staining the edges and corners darker than the rest of the piece. Sometimes a wash coat made of seven parts alcohol and one part four-pound-cut shellac, or a diluted lacquer thinner is put over a stain after it is dry to keep it from bleeding when the finish material is put over it.

FILLING

Fillers for wood finishes are optional; whether you use them depends on the wood you are finishing. Pine, cherry, basswood, poplar, fir, cedar and other small-pored, close-grained woods do not require any filler. Moderately open-pored woods such as birch, beech, gum and maple can accept a liquid filler. Open-pored woods, including oak, walnut and mahogany, ought to have a paste filler.

The object of a filler is to stuff the pores in the wood. You have to be careful not to rub it in too hard or it will come loose either on the spot or as soon as the finish is put over it. White zinc, white lead or a clear filler paste can be given a light pigment that will produce a blond finish, but in general the filler should either match or be a shade darker than the wood stain it is going over. When you are covering a wood stain, first apply a wash coat of thinned shellac to keep the stain from bleeding. Alternatively, you can put filler on wood before you stain it.

The paste fillers are considered a little better than the liquids at clogging wood pores, and most professionals prefer them. The paste is mixed with turpentine, benzine or naphtha until it has the consistency of heavy cream. Then mix whatever japan color you are using with turpentine until it reaches the proper shade and add that to the filler.

Rub the filler into the pores of the wood with a stiff brush, working both with and across the grain. Pay a lot of attention to the end grains, giving them an extra-heavy coating. After the filler is applied, rub it with a piece of burlap or other coarse cloth and wait for about 30 minutes before wiping off any excess that appears on the surface. Wipe across the grain, and use a light circular motion in the direction of the grain to blend in any cross-grain streaks. If you find a residue on the wood after the filler is completely dry, you can soften it with a rag soaked in turpentine and then scrape it off.

SEALING

Even close-grained woods will have soft spots that soak up finish material faster than the rest of the surface. Wood sealer is made to fill up the wood fibers, particularly in those soft spots. Almost any of the products on the market will do an adequate job on almost any wood. They all dry quickly and can be applied with either a brush or rag. It is best to wait 24 hours before giving the surface a light sanding, which will produce a satiny feel to the wood. The sealer prevents bleeding when applied over a stain and helps the finish material adhere.

While you can purchase ready-made sealers, you can also mix one part shellac to eight parts denatured alcohol and use it as a sealer in almost any situation. It dries quickly and provides excellent adhesion. In fact, diluted shellac is the *only* sealer to use over a penetrating oil stain. You can also dilute varnish by mixing it with an equal amount of turpentine. Or if you are finishing with lacquer and prefer not to use a commercial lacquer sealer, you can dilute the lacquer by mixing it 50-50 with lacquer thinner.

A sealer seals in everything, including any dust on the wood, so be sure the surface is dry and dust free before you brush the sealer into the wood.

GLAZING, DISTRESSING, ETC.

When you have stripped, sanded, stained, filled and sealed the wood, you have finally reached the point of putting on a finish coat. But if that coat is to have any special effects or overtones, now is the time to apply them.

Glazing

Glaze will allow you to shade, highlight or antique the wood, and it will also even out the color of a stain. There are several glazes on the market which come either tinted or clear so that you can add your own pigment. However, a normal method of glazing is simply to add a light tint to whatever stain or filler you are using. Another kind of glaze, which you can make yourself, consists of a tablespoon of artist's color, half a pint of turpentine and a tablespoon of lampblack. You can rub your glaze over the wood, then wipe most of it off except in corners, along edges or anywhere else you want the piece to appear worn. Whatever glaze you use, allow it to dry thoroughly and then seal it to the wood with a coat of thinned shellac.

Distressing

Distressing is a popular treatment among French and Italian cabinetmakers. You need some special implements which are probably already lying around your house, like an old mace. If you can't find your mace, a chunk of chain, pieces of coral or anything that will gouge and scratch the wood when you bang on it will do. First, you whack away at the wood until it is as marred as you want it to be. Then fill all the holes, gouges, scratches and digs with black glaze, dark stain, crayon, paint—anything that will make the piece look really aged. After that, you can put on your finish coats.

Etc.

Shading. This is accomplished by putting glaze or stain that is darker than the rest of the finish in the corners, along edges or wherever you want to give the piece highlights.

Splattering. You can splatter glaze or stain over the wood surface to produce a speckled finish. Be random but controlled about your splatters; use a stiff-bristled brush and be careful not to overload it, or you will get globs instead of speckles. Hold the brush over the work, bend the bristles back with a stick, and let go. With a little practice each splatter becomes a separate little elongated spot that looks just like a worm hole.

Finish Materials

Furniture is painted, varnished, shellacked, lacquered and enameled. All of these materials can be applied with a brush, roller or spray gun. Spraying is the preferred method for applying lacquer, while a brush or foam rubber pad will do just as well with shellac, varnish or paint.

SHELLAC

For centuries, shellac was the only finish cabinetmakers ever used. It has always been inexpensive, and is easily applied to create a smooth finish surface. However, it can be ruined with heat, water, alcohol and almost any chemical. It is a superb primer-sealer for any wood destined to be painted or varnished, although it will darken the wood.

Shellac is either white or orange and is a mixture of the resinous secretions of the Asian insect lac and denatured alcohol. The amount of lac used in a given can of shellac is indicated as its *cut*. A three-pound cut means that three pounds of lac were mixed with one gallon of alcohol. A five-pound cut would be five pounds of lac to one gallon of alcohol, and so forth. The shellac can usually has a chart that tells you how much alcohol to add in order to change the cut. That is fortunate because whatever cut you buy, you want to apply a one-pound cut to furniture. Don't buy any more than you will need in a relatively short period of time—the alcohol will evaporate quickly, and in any case the shelf life of shellac is no more than about a year.

Shellac is built up in thin coats that dry dust-free in about two hours, at which time you can sand it and apply the next coat. In shellacking casework, put three coats on the sides and at least five coats on the top.

Stir shellac. Shaking it causes bubbles that will stay on the wood and cause an uneven finish. Flow the shellac over wood with long, even strokes that overlap only slightly, and allow it to dry. Sand each coat lightly with superfine-grit abrasive or a fine grade of steel wool. Then wipe the surface with a tack rag and apply the next coat. Two coats are enough if you intend to varnish over the shellac; otherwise you can go on adding diluted coats until you have the glossy texture you want. If your last coat is too glossy, give it a light rubbing with fine steel wool until it dulls to a satiny sheen.

Do not apply shellac in temperatures under 65°F or on damp or humid days. If possible, use a new brush or foam rubber paint pad for each coat. If that many new brushes or pads are not feasible, clean your brush or pad with alcohol, then rinse it in a mild solution of ammonia and warm water.

LACQUER

Lacquer can be clear or have a pigment, and be glossy, semiglossy or flat. You have to be very specific about what you are going to put lacquer on and how you plan to apply it, because there are lacquers made for metals as well as wood, for brushing as well as spraying. You must use the sealer, and often the thinner, that is sold with the particular brand of lacquer you buy. The formulas for making lacquer are about as varied as the brand names.

Lacquer may outrank even varnish as the most-used finish material for furniture. It dries almost as it touches the wood and forms a thin coating that can be covered with a second application within minutes. The finish coats form a hard protection over wood that resist most liquids and temperature changes; the finish is also easy to rub down and repair. Lacquer is not as hard as the urethanes, however, and excessive moisture can cause it to peel.

Because lacquer dries so quickly, most people apply it with a spray gun.

To spray lacquer, you must thin it by about 50%. Keep your spray gun moving until the supply in its can is gone, or until you are finished painting. If you stop for more than a few moments, the lacquer will clog the gun nozzle, which will have to be cleaned in lacquer thinner. Each coat should be sanded lightly; expect to apply at least five coats if you are spraying. The final coat should be hand-rubbed.

When you are brushing on lacquer, use a soft-bristled brush and be swift. Work in long, overlapping strokes, and do not go back over the lacquer. Wait two hours for the material to harden, then sand it with a fine or superfine grit. After the third coat, there should be enough lacquer built up to hand-rub and polish.

VARNISH

Varnishes are durable and clear, and resist water, alcohol and most chemicals. You can still buy the old-fashioned, slow-drying, dust-collecting varnishes, but the urethanes are faster, stronger, quicker drying and easier to work with. The thing you cannot do with the urethanes is put them over shellac, lacquer or most general-purpose sander-fillers. There are, of course, primers for the urethanes which will do the same job of preparing your furniture to accept the varnish. You can also dilute whatever urethane you are using with an equal amount of turpentine, and use that as your primer.

The wood must be dust free and dry. If you never use a tack rag anywhere else, use it now to clean the wood surface before you varnish.

Never shake varnish; always stir it. Shaking causes bubbles which remain as the varnish dries, making the final surface rough. Flow varnish on the wood with a high-quality brush, a rag or a foam rubber paint pad. The pads are ideal because they hold a good amount of material and do not leave any brush strokes, which eliminates most of the difficulties of painting on varnish. Tap the bristles or pad against the rim of the can to get rid of excess varnish; dragging bristles across the rim produces bubbles.

If you are brushing on your varnish, use a minimum of long, overlapping strokes. Top off the work by going over it at right angles to your strokes with the tip of the bristles to get rid of any brush marks and achieve a uniform finish. It takes a while to develop the technique of "kissing" the top of a brush stroke, but once you learn how to do it, there will be no brush strokes showing in the final finish.

Each coat of varnish should be allowed to dry overnight and then sanded with a superfine-grit abrasive until all of the sheen is removed. Wipe away the dust with a tack rag and apply your second coat. If you have used a sealer, three applications of varnish should be enough, although each project will vary. Like every other coat, the final coat will have some rough spots caused by bubbles in the varnish and/or specks of dust. Don't let it bother you; this is what pumice, rottenstone, steel wool and wet/dry sandpaper are for, and one of them will give you exactly the finish you want.

ENAMEL

When you decide to paint furniture, you will almost always want to use an oil-based enamel. Enamel is varnish with a color added, so everything you now know about varnishing applies to painting with enamel. The same old bubbles will plague you unless you stir the enamel and pat the end of your brush against the can rather than dragging it over the rim. Brush with the grain as much as possible and top off your strokes by "kissing" them with the tip of the brush.

The process of enameling furniture is always the same. Sand the wood and wipe it with a tack rag. Apply a coat of filler or sealer (or both), and hand-sand it when it is dry. Wipe it with a tack rag and put on your primer. You don't have to do a perfect job here, but don't slobber and don't take any holidays. When it is dry, hand-sand the primer and wipe it clean with a tack rag. Now apply the first coat of enamel. When it is dry, give it a light hand sanding and wipe it clean with a tack rag. Two or, at most, three coats hand-sanded and cleaned between applications should be enough. About a month after the last coat is applied, give it a good coating of furniture wax.

Rubbing

Varnish, lacquer and shellac can all be rubbed after their final coats have had at least two days to dry and harden. All three materials tend to dry with blemishes from bubbles, dust or brush marks, giving the surface a rough feel and a less than perfect luster. To achieve a better luster, you can use the following materials:

Wet/dry sandpaper. This will produce a matte finish that is smooth and has a rather dull luster. You can use oil as the lubricant, but water is easier to apply and leaves no residue. The residue from oil can be removed with benzine. Soak a sheet of #500 wet/dry sandpaper in water or oil and wrap it around a sanding block. Using moderate pressure, work with the grain until the surface is smooth and even. Then wipe off any residue with a rag and clean water or, if you are using oil as your lubricant, clean with benzine.

Steel wool. A pad of steel wool will give you a satiny finish all by itself. If you use it with a light oil or paste wax, the finish will be even smoother and more lustrous. Use the finest grade of steel wool you can get, preferably #4/0, and rub only with the grain. Change pads as soon as they begin to fall apart, and do not rub too hard or you may go through the finish. Clean the surface with a soft cloth or, if you have been dipping the pad in oil or wax, clean the surface with benzine.

Rubbing compounds. These will deliver a high-gloss finish. You can use any of the furniture compounds or a fine-grade white automobile compound as long as it has no additives, including wax. Stay away from harsh or orange compounds.

Follow the instructions that come with the compound. In general, dampen a cloth, dip it in the compound and rub it into the surface with the grain. Wipe the surface clean at regular intervals until the finish is smooth. Then wipe it absolutely clean and sprinkle a little water on it. Using a clean cloth and very little compound, rub the surface until it is highly polished. Finish off with a rubbing of paste wax or pure lemon oil.

Pumice and rottenstone. Both are powders that will give you either a satin or a gloss finish, depending on the lubricant you use with them.

Wait at least seven days after the final finish coat has dried, then mix some FFF pumice with clean motor oil. You can really use any oil as long as it is not a drying oil. Dip a folded lint-free cloth into the paste and rub the surface with long, straight strokes along the grain. Keep sanding the surface until it is smooth and has lost most of its original luster; then wipe it clean.

Now comes the rottenstone, a finer powder than pumice. If you mix it with water you will get a gloss; with oil as its lubricant, you will get a satiny finish. Mix the lubricant with the rottenstone until you have a paste, then rub in on the surface with a lint-free cloth, maintaining moderate pressure. Rub until the surface squeaks and/or you have the luster you desire. Wipe the surface with a clean cloth.

A TRIO OF HAND-RUBBED FINISHES

If your persuasion is hard work and the glory of a hand-rubbed finish, you can find innumerable ways of refinishing a piece of furniture without ever lifting a brush or spray gun. It should be noted that everybody who does any hand rubbing has their own favorite materials and their own way of applying them. The procedure is likely to include some deep family secrets that have been handed down from generation to generation in the dead of a moonless night. To learn these secrets the best you can do is ask someone whose opinion you respect and take careful notes, then go home and do exactly what you were told to do. When that doesn't work, don't go back and ask for more information; deep family secrets are always imparted to outsiders with at least one important item conveniently omitted. So just take whatever you have of the formula and experiment; use parts of a lot of formulas until you find the way that works best for you. For what it's worth, here are three methods of hand-rubbing oil finishes that you can start with. Since they are all family secrets, each has a missing fact or two to protect the ancestral archives.

Tung Oil

The most important ingredient in varnish is tung oil. Tung oil is so good a preservative that the Chinese have used it for thousands of years to waterproof their clothing, boats and homes—it will seal anything from cloth to steel and masonry. It will also turn to jelly when it is exposed to air, so there is a problem storing it in a half-empty can. If you end up with half a can or less, put the oil in a smaller container or throw some stones into the can to fill up the air space. The oil will seal the stones but it won't solidify.

To apply, dip a cotton cloth into the tung oil and rub the cloth on the wood. Keep rubbing with the cloth or your bare hands until the oil has saturated the wood; then let it dry overnight. In the morning you will have a low-luster finish. If you rub in a second coat, you will get a medium luster and each coat after that will become glossier. You can stop whenever you reach the gloss you want. The secret, by the way, is that tung oil works best if you apply it on a dry, warm day or in a heated room.

Linseed Oil

Always use boiled linseed oil, never raw linseed oil, on furniture. "Boiled" means that it has drying agents in it; raw linseed oil hardly ever dries. Exactly how you apply linseed oil to wood is strictly a matter of who you talk to; ask three furniture finishers, and you will get at least five opinions. Here is a basic procedure that works for some people:

1. Mix two parts boiled linseed oil with one part turpentine or mineral spirits.

2. Place the open can over a fire, or put it in a pan of boiling water. Make sure the can is open, or it will open itself with a loud bang.

3. When the linseed oil is hot, dip a lint-free rag in it and rub the oil into a small area of the wood. Keep rubbing the same spot for about 15 or 20 minutes. You can use your bare hands.

4. When the area is completely saturated, wipe any excess oil off the surface with a clean rag.

5. Reheat the linseed oil and proceed to saturate the next small section of wood. Be sure to dig all excess oil out of the corners and crevices of the project, where it will eventually become sticky or harden.

6. Twenty-four hours after the first coat is applied, rub in the second coat (some experts recommend waiting a week between each coat). Apply a minimum of three coats; the more coats, the more lustrous the finish.

7. Every six months or so during the entire lifetime of the piece, rub a new coat of linseed oil into the wood.

Caution: Always burn, bury or sink the rags you use with linseed oil. They are highly combustible and should never be left lying around your house.

French Polish

The French polish is a variation on the linseed oil finish, and produces a very high gloss. There are several ways to French-polish; this is one of them:

1. Soak a grapefruit-sized wad of lint-free rags in hot boiled linseed oil. Squeeze out the ball and dip it in a can of one-pound-cut shellac.

2. Rub the ball of rags on the wood as if the rags were a belt sander. The ball should be moving as it touches the surface and keep moving for as long as it is on the wood. Use enough pressure so that the oil and shellac are pressed into the wood, but not so much that the rags stick. When the wad is dry, work your way off the edge of the furniture without stopping until it is clear of the surface.

3. Allow the project to dry for 24 hours before putting on a second coat. You can add a coat every 24 hours for the rest of your life, and each coat will be glossier than the one before it. If it becomes too glossy, tone it down with pumice and motor oil.

WAXES AND LEMON OIL

Waxing is a nice way to polish any new finish. The trouble with waxing furniture is that the old wax must be cleaned off before a new coat is put on. And almost nobody bothers to clean off old wax, so it builds up on the furniture finish, dulling the luster, becoming gummy and finally making the original finish look as if it needs to be stripped. This is why it is always a good idea to thoroughly clean a piece with benzine before you decide it absolutely must be restored or refinished.

Pure lemon oil—not lemon oil with beeswax, linseed oil or silicone added—will preserve furniture far better than any wax. Pure lemon oil cannot be put over wax. It picks up dirt and deposits it on the cloth, so it is really a cleanser, but it will also fill between the wood fibers and protect them from absorbing moisture. Lemon oil is not greasy, but any excess should be wiped off since it will not evaporate and the wood will not absorb much of it. It should be rubbed into the finish about once a month, and should be applied to unfinished portions about once a year to protect the wood.

RESEATING: SPLINTS, RUSH AND CANING

If the seat in a chair or sofa is not upholstered or made of a solid material (wood, plastic or metal), it is probably made of woven ash splints, rush or cane. All of these materials will wear after years of being sat on; they can break or will become tattered and have to be replaced. The actual work involved requires very few tools and demands nothing more than considerable patience applied to specific procedures.

Splints

Probably the most common type of seating material used by our forebears was the ash splint. It was common because ash trees abounded in the Early American forests, and the splints could be obtained by stripping the annular rings from logs and cutting them into strips ¾" wide. Today, machine-made ash splints are sold in 6' lengths with widths of ⅝" or ¾". In order to reseat an average chair you will need about 15 ash splints plus a pail, some heavy twine, scissors, a utility knife, a brush and tung oil or boiled linseed oil.

Soak the ash splints in warm water for at least 10 minutes before weaving them into a seat. The splints must be put on the seat so that their smooth side can be seen. You will find that when you bend a wet splint one side is smooth and the opposite side has tiny splinters that make it feel rough. Always keep the smooth side facing you as you wrap the splint around the rails of the chair. The smooth side must also be out whenever you are joining the ends of a splint.

MAKING SPLINT JOINTS

For the sake of both appearance and strength, the joints in a splint seat are always made in the underside of the seat. The procedure for making a joint involves only a utility knife and scissors:

1. Three inches from the end of one splint, use your scissors to cut a triangular notch out of each side to create a tapered neck that looks like an arrowhead (see illustration).

2. Three inches from the end of the joining splint, use your utility knife to cut a triangle out of the center of the splint that is just wide enough at its base to accept the neck of the arrowhead. The triangle need only be as long as the width of the splint. You may find the safest way of making it is to use your knife to cut the with-grain sides, then force the tab upward and clip off its base with scissors.

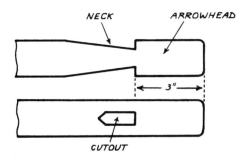

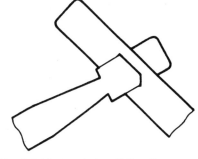

The arrowhead and triangle create a way of locking splint ends together.

The joint is made by sliding the arrowhead through the triangle and rotating the splints into a straight line.

3. Interlock the two ends by sliding the arrowhead into the triangle at right angles, then twist it around so that the two splints align.

During the course of reseating you will have to join several splints into long, continuous strips. Always be careful to make your joints so that the smooth side of the splints are facing outward.

THE PROCESS OF WEAVING

The splints must be soaked in warm water for about 10 minutes until they become pliable enough to bend around the rails of the chair. Place three or four splints in the water to begin with; each time you remove one, put a new one in its place.

The most common pattern used in weaving ash splints is known as the diagonal weave, and it's done as follows:

1. Temporarily tie one end of your first splint to the side rail of the chair with heavy twine. Loop the other end of the splint around the top of the front rail, bring it up behind the back rail and continue turning it over the rails.

2. When you reach the end of the splint, cut a 3″-long arrowhead in the end and notch the end of the next splint to join it.

3. Continue wrapping and joining splints until the width of the chair is covered, then tie the free end of the last splint to the side rail of the chair. The splints swell as the water soaks into them, and they will shrink as they dry out again. They should be wrapped around the chair rails just tightly enough so that you can depress them about ½″ if the chair is small and 1″ if it is large. When you have finished wrapping the rails front to back, the splints should all lie evenly next to each other and all be perpendicular to the side rails, with a uniform tension—that is, when you depress each strand it should be no looser than any other strand.

4. To weave the first splint side-to-side, wrap one end around the side rail, and weave it back through the front-to-back splints in the underside of the seat. The other end is brought around the side rail and tucked between the front-to-back splints. Join a new splint to the free end and continue weaving according to the diagonal weave pattern illustrated until the entire seat is woven.

The splints dry quickly and the front-to-back strands become tighter and tighter as you work, making it difficult to weave the side-to-side splints between them. You can use a scrap piece of splint to push the splints over and under the front-to-back strands.

5. Chair seats are often splayed, which means that when you are finished weaving there will still be triangular sections at each side that must be filled

The diagonal weave. Note that the pattern repeats starting with every fifth cross row.

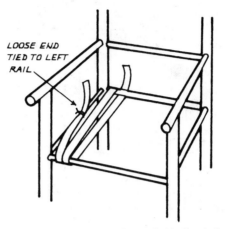

Tie the end of your first splint to the left chair rail, then wrap the splint around the front and back rails.

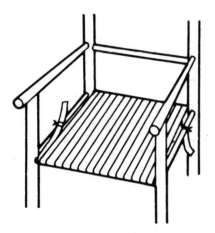

Join the splints under the chair seat and tie the last splint to the right chair rail.

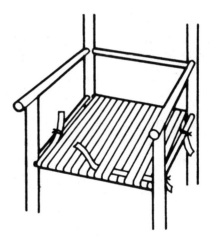

Tuck the short end of the side-to-side splint between the front-to-back splints.

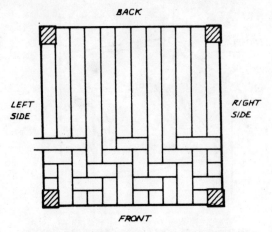

Weave the side-to-side splints according to this pattern, repeating the pattern starting with every fifth row.

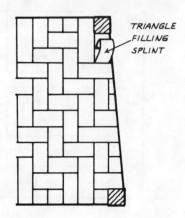

The unwoven triangles in a splayed seat are filled with separate, short splints which have their short ends tucked under the weave.

with extra splints. Weave the splints from the front rail to the back upright and tuck the short end under the weaving. Then wrap the splint around the front rail and weave it back to the post; cut it at the post and tuck the end into the weave.

6. There still may be an unwoven triangular area between the front rail and about halfway to the back of the seat. Wrap a short splint around the front rail and weave it on both the top and underside of the seat, then tuck the ends into the weave at whatever point the gap ends. You may have to notch the splint so that it will fit snugly against the front corner post.

7. When the seat is completely woven, trim off any rough edges or splinters and allow the splints to dry completely before applying any finish material. Since ash splints are a hardwood, you can stain them if you wish; but give them a coat of tung oil or boiled linseed oil to preserve and seal the wood.

Rush

Rush is made from any of several wetlands plants, principally the leaves of cattails, which are soaked and twisted together into long strands that can

SQUARE KNOT

CLOVE HITCH

HALF HITCH

The square knot is used to tie lengths of rush together. The clove hitch is used to tie the rush temporarily to a chair rung. The half hitch is used to knot the rush securely when tying it off.

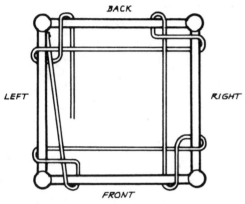

The basic weave. The rush is always looped around the chair rails in this configuration.

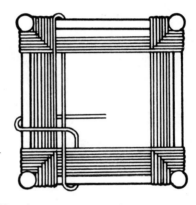

Weaving a square seat.

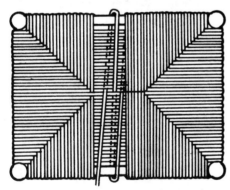

With a rectangular seat, the center section is filled in with a series of figure eight loops that go around the front and back rails and cross through the space between the two center side-to-side strands.

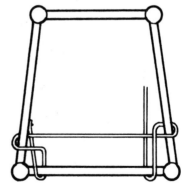

The corners in a splayed seat must first be filled with short lengths of rush tacked to the side rails.

then be woven to form the seat of a chair. Natural rush is still available but it is difficult to work with. Most rerushing done today employs one of the many rush substitutes on the market.

The primary rush substitute is kraft paper twisted into uniform strands, although several synthetic materials in various diameters and colors, such as plastic, are also used. All can be purchased in seat-length spools, balls or hanks at upholstery supply houses. You can also use any strong string or small rope, and weave it into a rush pattern.

Most chair seats are either splayed or rectangular, and each corner must be filled with rush. Unlike working with ash splints, you have to begin at the corners and fill in the unwoven center area last. In order to do any rushing you will need a piece of wood, screwdriver or a dull knife to use as a regulator to push the rush tightly in place. You should also know how to tie three common sailor's knots—the square knot, clove hitch and half hitch.

THE BASIC WEAVE

For an absolutely square chair seat, use the basic weave until the seat is completely filled. Work with lengths of about 15′ or 20′ which you tie together with a square knot. Tack one end of the rush under the left chair rail beside the back corner post. You can untwist the cord just enough to insert the tack between the strands. Bring the rush up and over the top of the front chair rail, then around the top of the left rail and across the top of the right rail. Continue from the right rail over the top of the front rail, then over the top of the back rail, the right rail, and then the left rail. From the left rail, loop the rush over the top of the back rail and bring it forward to beside your starting point at the front rail. Continue looping the rush around all four corners of the chair in the same pattern, always keeping the cord taut and the tension uniform.

Rectangular Seats

A rectangular seat is woven with the basic weave until the side rails are completely covered. At this point, there will still be a portion in the center. This is closed with figure eight loops over the front and back rails. The rush always crosses from top to bottom through the same opening between the center two side-to-side rows.

Splayed Seats

Rushing the splayed seat commonly found in chairs requires some variations in technique since the larger front corners must be woven first. Follow this procedure:

1. Cut a length of rush about 4′ long and tack one end to the left rail near the front corner post. Loop the free end over the front rail, both side rails and finally the front rail next to the right corner post. Tack the end of the rush to the right rail. The cord should be taut, and the tacks on each rail should be the same distance from the corner posts. Cut the cord so that ½″ remains beyond the tacks.

2. Cut a second piece of rush and tack one end to the left rail; the tack should be an inch or so behind the first tack. Now weave the second strand around the rails, keeping the rush taut, and tack it to the right rail, 1″ behind the first tack.

3. After you have tacked five or six rows around the front corners, push the rush together with your piece of wood to make certain they are woven together as tightly as you can get them. Continue weaving the front corners until the distance between the corners is equal to the length of the back chair rail. By this time your tacks should have been spaced along the side rails so that the last tacks are close the back corner posts. Now you have a square area to be filled using the continuous basic weave.

4. Cut a 15′ or 20′ length of rush and tack or tie one end to the left rail near the back post, then bring it up to the front rail, around the left and right rails, back to the front rail, then to the rear rail, around the right and left rails and over the back rail again, to complete the first strand of the continuous weave. Push the rush tightly into each corner, keeping as much tension on it as you can muster. Whenever you must add more rush, tie the ends together with a square knot underneath the seat; this will be buried inside the weave. Whenever you have to stop working, lead the free end of the rush down to any of the chair rungs and tie it tightly with a clove hitch so that the tension in the seat remains constant. Stop after every five or six rows and tie the rush to a chair rung, then use your regulator to push the strands tightly together at each corner. You want to keep every strand parallel to the seat rails.

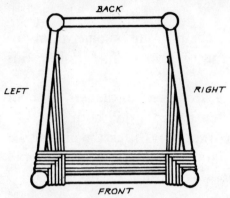

The tacks along the side rails of a splayed seat should be evenly spaced and opposite each other so that an absolute square is created in the center of the seat. The distance between the last weave on the front rail should equal the width of the back rail.

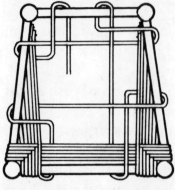

Fill in the square hole in the center of the splayed seat with the basic continuous weave.

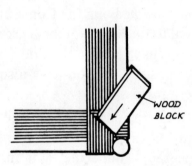

After every five or six rows of weaving, stop to push the strands tightly together with your regulator.

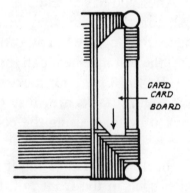

Fill in the space between your weave with pieces of cardboard that are cut at an angle and pushed into the corners of the seat. The cardboard padding can be put on both the top and bottom of the seat.

5. When you have completed several rows of the continuous weave, cut angles in both ends of a piece of cardboard and insert a pointed end into the front corners between the rush. The cardboard should be as close in color to the rush as you can find; its purpose is to give the seat a modicum of padding but also to separate the strands so that they will not chafe against each other or wear out against the rails of the chair. You can turn the chair upside down

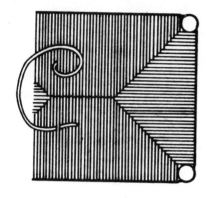

Tie off the last strand with a half hitch and tuck the free end of the strand inside the weave.

and insert cardboard into the corners on the underside of the seat for even more protection. When the sides of the seat have been woven enough to accept padding, insert pieces of cardboard between the rush on one or both sides of the seat.

6. When the sides have been completely covered, bring the end of the rush from the left rail, and up through the space between the two center side-to-side strands Tie a strand to the end of the rush that is long enough to complete the center opening.

7. The center opening is filled with a series of tightly compacted figure eights which loop over the top of the front rail, come up through the space between the two center strands, then loop over the top of the back rail and emerge through the center again. Press each strand tightly against the other strands with your regulator. The last strand in the seat is brought up through the center, looped around the front rail and tied to itself with several half hitches underneath the seat. Be careful to maintain tension on the rush until you have secured the first half hitch. You can then add three or four more hitches and hide the knot between the strands.

8. Rub the flat side of your regulator over the edges of the chair rails to make certain none of the strands is higher than the rest of the weave. Now give the seat a coating of tung oil on both the top and underside of the seat. Allow the oil to dry for 15 to 20 minutes, then wipe off any excess. Let the oil dry overnight before using the chair.

Caning

Caning is the weaving of rattan cane strips into chair seats or backs. It can be done by weaving strands of cane through holes in the frame or by wedging prewoven webbing into grooves routed out of the furniture wood. Cane is a hard, glossy bark taken from the rattan palm and sliced into narrow strips.

To put prewoven webbing on a chair all you need is scissors, a mallet, glue, a wooden wedge, a utility knife, a pail, a craft knife and some hardwood splines (or wedging).

PREWOVEN WEBBING

Cane that has been woven by machine comes in several widths, ranging from 8″ to 36″, and in any length within reason. Most furniture suppliers also offer several patterns to choose from. Buy enough webbing so that you have at least 2″ more than the dimensions of the seat on all sides. You also need enough spline to fit into the groove around the perimeter of the seat. Measure the width and depth of the groove carefully, or take a piece of the old spline with you to be sure you get the proper size. If you want to match the old webbing pattern, take a piece of that with you as well. When you have removed the old webbing and cleaned out the grooves around the seat, follow this procedure:

1. Soak the webbing in nearly boiling water for about 10 minutes, or until the rattan is pliable.

2. Lay the webbing over the seat and position it so that at least ½″ of webbing extends beyond all four grooves. If you have more than ½″ of webbing, cut it off with your scissors.

3. Drive the webbing into the grooves, making certain the shiny side is up. You can put glue in the grooves either before or after you insert the webbing, using any good furniture glue such as a casein, urea, liquid hide, cream or white. Since you are filling a narrow groove, you may find it is easier to choose a glue that comes in a plastic bottle rather than one that must be mixed and then poked into the slot with a stick.

Begin along the front edge of the webbing and push 3″ or 4″ of webbing into the groove using a wooden wedge and your mallet. (An ideal wedge for this purpose is half of a spring clothespin.) Now push 2" or 3" of webbing into the center of the back groove and into the centers of both sides, keeping as uniform a tension on the webbing as you can. Continue hammering the webbing until it is completely seated in its grooves. Work from the center of each side outward, alternating between opposite sides so that the tension will remain constant.

4. With all of the webbing in its grooves, use a craft knife to trim off whatever excess extends above the groove.

5. Soak the spline in hot water until it is pliable. If you have put glue in the grooves before inserting the webbing, you may want to add more so that glue will ooze out of the groove when the spline is pushed into it. If you did not use any glue, inject it in the grooves now.

Working with prewoven webbing. (A) Drive the webbing into its groove with a wooden wedge, such as half a spring clothespin. (B) Hammer the spline into the groove. (C) Trim off excess webbing inside the groove with a craft knife.

6. If the corners of the seat allow you to bend the spline around them, use a single piece of the wedging, and begin in the center of any side by hammering the spline into the groove with its narrow edge down. If the corners are sharp, cut four pieces of spline to fit into each side and meet at the corners with a miter joint. When you have hammered the spline into its grooves, it should be level with the surface of the chair wood. Immediately wipe off all excess glue with a damp rag or sponge.

7. You will discover some hairlike fuzz on the webbing. You can sand it off with a fine or superfine-grit abrasive. You can also burn it off with a propane torch, provided the cane is still wet. Use the coolest blue flame you can produce and keep it moving quickly over the cane so that it only singes the fuzz. If you hold the flame in place for any length of time it will change the color of the rattan and also burn it.

8. When the cane has dried, it should have also shrunk sufficiently to give you a taut chair seat. You can darken it with a diluted stain and/or give it a gloss by applying shellac, varnish, or lacquer. Alternatively, you can simply preserve it with a coat of tung oil or boiled linseed oil.

WEAVING CANE

When the frame you want to recane has holes instead of grooves around the seat area, you have to handweave strands of rattan to form the seat. Measure the hole diameter and the spacing between holes to determine the largest width of cane that you can use. If you choose to create a delicate or elaborate weave, you can use smaller cane or even strands of different widths. Follow this guide to ascertain what cane size you need:

Hole Diameter	Hole Spacing	Cane Size
1/8"	3/8"	Carriage and Superfine
3/16"	1/2"	Fine-Fine
3/16"	5/8"	Fine
1/4"	3/4"	Medium
5/16"	7/8"	Common

Strand cane is sold in hanks of 1,000′ ranging from superfine to common, each of which is between 6′ and 10′ in length. The hank also includes a wider strand called a binder, which is used to form an edging around the weave when you are finished. You will need about 250′ of cane to reseat an average-sized chair seat. You also need a supply of golf tees or caning pegs to hold the ends of the strands while you are weaving, scissors, a pail, an awl, and a bodkin (needle) or two. You can buy a bodkin with an eye in one end at any furniture supply store; it is used to thread strands through the weave. You can make a blunt wire bodkin to separate strands by cutting a piece of coat hanger and bending the last ½″ of one of its ends.

Cane strands have a rough side and a shiny side. Always keep the shiny side up, and as you weave try to maintain a uniform tension that allows you to depress each strand no less than ½″ and no more than ¾″. When you are weaving a splayed seat you may find it necessary to skip some of the holes in the frame in order to keep all of your strands parallel, but all of the holes will eventually be filled in. Your primary concern during each of the weaving stages is to keep the glossy side of each strand facing outward and to make sure each row is parallel to all the other rows.

The process described here is for making the standard octagonal weave. Place all the rattan you intend to use in a pail of hot water for 10 or 15 minutes. If the water is not hot, the cane will still become pliable enough to work with, but it will require about an hour and a half to get that way. You can keep all of the strands in water until you are ready to use them.

1. Remove the first strand from your pail of water and push 4″ of it down through the top of the center hole in the front of the seat. Shove a golf tee into the hole until it wedges the strand in place. Stretch the strand across the top of the seat frame and insert it through the center hole in the back rail, then bring it up through the hole immediately to the right. Extend the strand to the front of the seat and down the first hole to the right of the center and up the next hole. Keep on stretching the rattan across the top of the frame and crossing it under the chair to the adjacent hole so that the rows are all parallel. When you reach the end of the strand, poke it down the last hole and push a golf tee into the hole to hold the strand in place. If the seat is splayed, skip whatever holes you have to in the back and right side to keep the rows parallel. When you have covered the right side of the chair, do the left side: peg a new strand in the first hole to the left of the center hole in the back rail, bring the strand to the front and continue as above until the entire seat has been covered. (See page 108, A and B.)

A

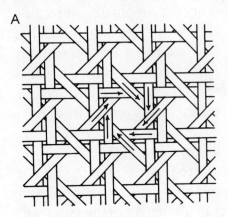

The standard octagonal weave pattern.

B

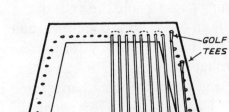

Start by pegging your first strand in the center hole of the front rail. By keeping the front-to-back strands parallel you will skip some of the holes in the side rail.

C

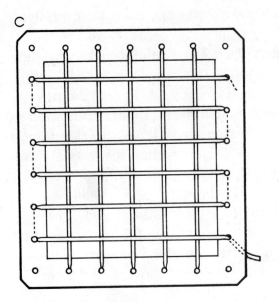

The first side-to-side strands cross <u>over</u> the front-to-back strands.

D

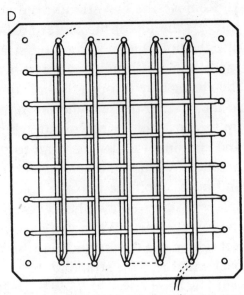

The second front-to-back strands cross <u>over</u> the side-to-side strands.

E

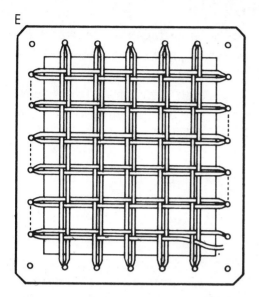

The second side-to-side strands go <u>under</u> the first row of front-to-back strands and <u>over</u> the second row of front-to-back strands.

F

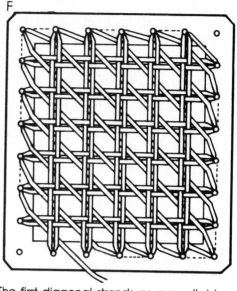

The first diagonal strands go <u>over</u> all side-to-side strands and <u>under</u> all front-to-back strands.

G

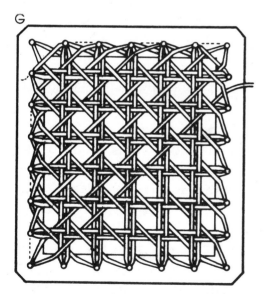

The second diagonal strands go <u>over</u> the front-to-back strands and <u>under</u> the side-to-side strands.

H

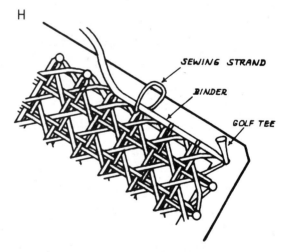

SEWING STRAND

BINDER

GOLF TEE

Loop the sewing strand over the binder and return it through the same hole, then cross under the chair rail to the next hole.

2. Starting at any hole next to a corner hole, peg the free end of a strand and lay a series of side-to-side strands *over* the front to back rows. Always cross to the next hole by going underneath the chair frame, keeping the shiny side of the strand upward, and maintaining a constant tension. Always leave 4″ of strand extending through any hole that you are pegging so that you will have enough material to form a knot when you are ready to tie off the strands. (See page 108, C.)

3. Now start all over again, stretching a second series of strands from front to back. This new layer goes *over* the side-to-side rows and enters the same holes used by your first front-to-back rows. The holes are big enough so that you can push the second layer to one side of the first weave. Be sure that each row is on the same side of the first weave. (See page 108, D.)

4. Now the real weaving begins. Working from left to right, carry each strand *under* the first row of front-to-back strands (step 1) and *over* the second row of front-to-back strands (step 3). You are adding a second weave to the side-to-side holes; keep the strands to the same side of the holes. When you have finished, your seat should appear to be a series of double-rowed boxes. The strands should be parallel or at right angles to each other with their shiny sides facing upward. Note that so far, you have not put any strands into tbe four corner holes. If the squares are not square, this is a good time to straighten them. Also check the uniformity of tension in the strands. You can remove one tee at a time and pull on the 4″ pigtail to tighten the strands. (See page 109, E.)

5. Start the first diagonal weave in any hole you wish. The strand is consistently passed *over* all side-to-side strands and *under* all front-to-back strands. You can use your blunt wire bodkin to separate strands; use the threaded eyed bodkin to carry the strand between the first four weaves. (See page 109, F.)

6. The second diagonal weave runs at right angles to the first (step 5) and passes *over* the front-to-back strands and *under* the side-to-side strands. When you are finished, your chair seat will have a series of regular octagons in it. If they are not all identical, push a tee through them to straighten them out. (See page 109, G.)

7. Turn the chair upside down and tie off all the loose ends by pushing the free end of the strand under the weave, looping it around and pulling the end through the loop until it is tight. Trim the pigtail to a length of 1". When you have tied all the ends you can remove the tees from their holes.

8. The binder is used to cover all but the four corner holes and provide a neat protection against wear at the edges. The binder should be wide enough to cover the holes, and is sewn into each hole with narrow pieces of cane. Cut enough binder to go around the edge of the seat or, if the seat has sharp corners, use separate strands from corner hole to corner hole. Taper the last ¼" of the binder and push it down through one of the corner holes, then peg it. Tie a knot in one end of the strand you are using to sew on the binder; pull the strand up through the bottom of the hole next to the corner until the knot almost catches on the underside of the hole. Loop the sewing strand over the binder and push the strand back down through the same hole. Cross under the chair frame to the next hole (or skip every other hole) and bring it up again. Loop it over the binder and back down the hole again. Continue sewing all the way around the weaving. When you are finished, tie off the loose ends of the binder and sewing strand. (See page 109, H.)

When you are finished weaving, check the uniformity of your pattern, using an awl or golf tee to straighten any misaligned holes. Also sand or burn off any furriness (see page 106). When the rattan has dried, it should be sealed on both sides with a coating of tung oil or boiled linseed oil. You can also stain, shellac, varnish or lacquer a handwoven cane seat.

UPHOLSTERY: SPRINGS, WEBBING AND BURLAP

Upholstered furniture can be overstuffed, or have pads or spring seats. Overstuffed chairs and sofas may be comprised of springs sewn in their cushions as well as in their seats and backs. Padded furniture has webbing or a solid base that supports cushions. Spring seats rely on webbing tacked to the frame which supports springs that are either sewn or clipped in place. You can, of course, encounter pieces of furniture that use features of all three.

When you are replacing the covering on upholstered furniture, you will need to purchase muslin, batting and glazed cotton as well as the cover fabric. The basic tools you will need include a magnetic hammer; a ripping tool; a webbing stretcher; webbing and upholstery tacks; straight and curved upholstery needles; and upholstery pins.

Taking Upholstery Apart

If you are intent on completely dismantling the upholstered part of a piece of furniture, you will be more comfortable if you rest the piece on an elevated work stand or on sawhorses. Start with the piece upside down, and use a mallet and tack ripper to pry loose all tacks holding the dustcover and skirt from the underside of the frame. Try to save all of the fabric pieces so you can use them as patterns for cutting new fabric. It is also a good idea to make a sketch of the furniture and key it according to the pieces you take off it. You are going to wind up with a pile of cloth, all of which is different in texture and shape, and trying to remember where each one goes can become confusing.

When you have removed all the tacks you can find underneath the frame, right the piece and continue pulling tacks. Make copious notes to yourself as you remove the cover, particularly about how it is fitted around corners and posts and how the various pieces are joined. When you have removed the cover, glazed cotton padding, muslin undercover, padding, edge roll and burlap, you will be left with the springs, which are attached to the webbing.

Springs

The most common furniture springs are the coil compression type, which are manufactured in a whole range of diameters, heights and gauges. There are also numerous sizes of coil extension springs which are attached to the frames of many beds and hold metal straps that cross the frame opening. Many manufacturers also use nonsagging zigzag springs because they are less expensive than coil springs.

Coil compression springs function according to the thickness of the wire gauge, how the metal was tempered and the shape of the spring itself. Generally speaking, the thicker the wire, the stiffer the spring; but springs used in upholstery are sometimes designated as OBE (open both ends); KBE (knotted both ends) or KOE (knotted one end). OBE and KOE springs are normally used for backs; and KBE springs are put in cushions, but there are no laws that say they cannot be interchanged to achieve a particular height or hardness.

Springs can—and do—wear out. To test a spring, place it on a flat, hard surface and push straight down on it with quick, continuous up-and-down pressure. If the spring compresses evenly, it is still usable. If it sways to one side, folds in the center or twists out of shape, it should be replaced.

You may not be able to locate an exact duplicate of the springs you want to replace, in which case you have three choices: 1) You can get the next taller, next grade softer spring and tie it down to the height you want. 2) You can use the next shorter, next grade harder and don't tie it as much as the other springs. 3) You can take the next taller, next grade harder and "run it in."

"Running in" a spring will both shorten and soften it. Push the free end of the coil under the next lower coil, and then twist the spring so that the crossed section slides down under each succeeding coil until it reaches the bottom of the spring. This is easy to do with either end of an OBE spring. But with KOE springs you can work with only the unknotted end. You will have to unwrap or cut one of the knots in a KBE spring for this operation.

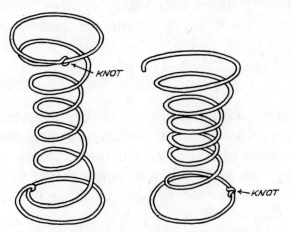

Any spring can be shortened by "running it in"—forcing the top coil under the next lower coil and twisting the crossed section down to the bottom of the spring.

Webbing

There are only two ways of supporting springs: on the frame itself or on some kind of webbing. The frame is used whenever a low-profile spring such as one found on a cot is required. Attachment of the springs to the frame is usually done with a clip which is screwed to the frame.

Webbing can be metal, wood or, most usually, fabric. Always use the best grade of jute webbing available. For backs and arms, use 3"-wide webbing; seats require a width of 3½″ or 4″. Whatever its width, the webbing is held to the frame with barbed webbing tacks. Webbing tacks are sold in several weights, but most often the 12-ounce (#12) or 14-ounce (#14) sizes are used. If you cannot find webbing tacks, use the next larger size upholstery tack.

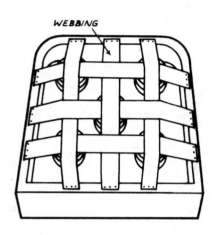

WEBBING

Webbing is evenly spaced and woven at right angles across the bottom of the furniture, then tacked to the bottom rails.

ATTACHING THE WEBBING

Fabric webbing must be spaced, stretched and tacked at right angles across the center of the frame. The spacing between your webbing on the frame should be between ½″ and 1″ (a good compromise is ¾″). There is no strength advantage to overlapping the edges of webbing, and in fact the overlap will cause the tacking ends to be lumpy. Mark the front rail—the top for a pad seat, the underside for a spring seat; then do the back and side rails, bearing in mind that you want all of the webbing to cross the frame hole at right angles and be evenly spaced.

Do not cut off pieces of the webbing—most stretchers need a considerable excess of webbing to grip. Fold over 1½″ of the free end and tack it ½″ from the front edge of the rail, staggering seven tacks so that no two of them are in the same grain line of the frame. The ½″ allowance is to keep the wood from splitting and to give you enough space to tack on the edge roll and the cover materials. It helps if you draw a pencil or chalk line ½″ inside the outside edges of all four rails before you begin tacking.

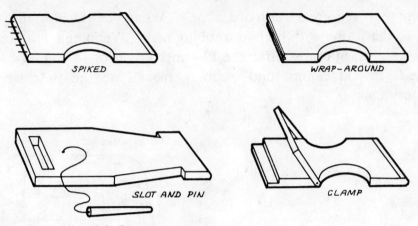

SPIKED

WRAP-AROUND

SLOT AND PIN

CLAMP

Webbing stretchers all work in the same manner.

With one end tacked, pull the webbing taut over the frame and line it up over the opposite rail. Hold the cushioned end of your webbing stretcher against the outside of the frame, angle it upward 30° to 45°, then grip the webbing. Hold the cushioned end of the stretcher against the rail with one hand, and slowly push the webbing down with your other hand at the gripping end of the stretcher. The webbing will tighten, then pop as the stretcher reaches its parallel position. Test the tautness of the webbing by pushing down on it with your hand or bouncing a hammer on it. The strip ought to give somewhat, but not produce a noticeable bulge.

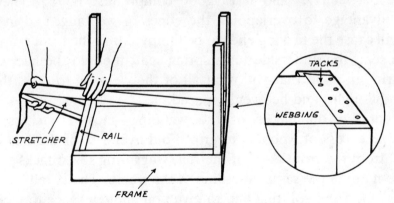

STRETCHER

RAIL

FRAME

TACKS

WEBBING

Brace the cushioned end of the stretcher against the frame at about a 45° angle and insert the webbing in its free end. Push down on the stretcher until the webbing pops and is taut against the rail. Tack the webbing.

If the tautness is correct, drive four tacks through the webbing and into the frame ½″ from the edge. Cut the webbing 1½″ from the tacks and fold it over, leaving ½″ of uncovered wood on the frame. Then tack the flap with three tacks staggered between the first four.

Install the front-to-back webbing first, then interweave the side-to-side strips.

SLACK WEBBING

Seats that are meant to be round or saddle-shaped give you the feeling of sinking into the padding rather than sitting on it. To achieve this rounded effect, stretch the webbing across the seat frame and tack it, but do not use your stretcher. If the seat bottom is to have a specific curve, drape the webbing in whatever shape you desire and then tack it. Because the webbing in both instances is not truly taut, it will tend to slide out of position unless you sew together each of the crossovers.

METAL AND WOOD WEBBING

You can buy metal webbing made of heavy-gauge steel wire with springs permanently attached to it. You can also get perforated steel straps that permit the springs to be attached to them at any point you desire. Usually the preformed metal webbing is made to order for a furniture manufacturer, so it is difficult to replace it. However, you can use the perforated straps to reinforce it, or, for that matter, to reinforce fabric webbing.

Wooden webbing can actually be a full plate of wood running across the bottom of the frame and supporting the springs, or it can be a series of slats (usually running side to side) that support either springs or simply a mattress. Anytime metal springs are joined to wood, they will squeak and groan. If you are attaching springs to wood, place jute webbing, layers of burlap or wads of cotton between the metal and wood to keep them quiet.

WEBBING FOR BACKS AND ARMS

Backs and arms framed to accept coil springs should be webbed in exactly the same way as seats, although you can use 3″-wide instead of 3½″ or 4″ webbing. You can also spread the webbing 2″ to 4″ apart. Be careful as you apply the webbing that the back or arm can stand the pressure of the fabric.

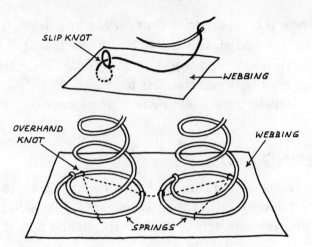

Springs should be stitched to the webbing at three or four points.

Both backs and arms tend to be more fragile than seat frames, and you want to be sure the webbing does not twist them out of shape. Also try to plan your cross-webbing so that it falls behind the base of each spring—that is, the spring should be attached to an intersection in the webbing whenever possible.

Putting on the Springs

The process of attaching springs involves sewing the springs to the webbing and tying them down, then covering them with burlap and tacking a felt edge roll around the frame. Stuffing is then placed on the burlap and covered with a layer of muslin.

With a double-pointed needle and #60 six-ply tying twine, start tying at any of the corner springs to the webbing. Tie a slipknot in the end of the twine and push your needle down through the top of the webbing, then up again to bring the needle through your slipknot and tighten it. Draw the twine around the base of the spring and down through the webbing. Stretch the twine under the webbing to a second point on the spring, then bring it up and around the spring again. Every spring should be tied with an overhand knot in at least three places—preferably four—with the last knot positioned nearest the next spring. If you are tying a spring to a crossover in the webbing, the most obvious places to knot the spring are at the four corners of the intersection. When you have completed tying the first spring, carry the twine under the webbing to the next spring and continue tying until all of the springs are attached to the webbing. Tie off the end of the twine with several half hitches around the base of the last spring.

TYING DOWN THE COILS

There are two ways of tying down springs to form either a tight-spring seat or a spring-edge seat.

Tight-Spring Seats

Tight-spring seats can have either rounded or flat surfaces and are attached to the webbing of the chair or sofa. They are most often found in furniture that is not fully upholstered and has no loose cushions.

When you are making a tight-spring seat, you have to do a little thinking ahead before you tie the springs to your webbing. Your first consideration is to determine the height of the finished seat so that you can gauge how high the springs should stand. Figure the height of the finished seat from the floor to the top of its cover. Now subtract about an inch to allow for the padding and cover. Then measure the distance from the webbing to the floor and subtract that from your overall height. The result is the height of the springs *after* they have been tied down. Suppose you have a 6″ space for your springs. If you buy 6″ springs, they will give you a maximum of resilience. If you use 7″ or 8″ springs and tie them down (compress them) to 6″, you will have less resilience.

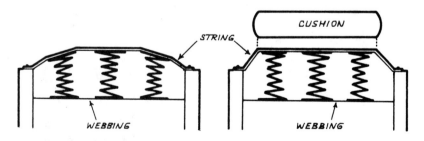

Seats that have cushions will have their springs tied flat. Uncushioned seats have their springs rounded.

Never tie down a spring more than 2″ below its natural height or it will give you no resilience at all. It will also put too much pressure on the webbing and the fabric over it, as well as be somewhat uncomfortable to sit on.

If the furniture has closed arms and back, the seat springs must be tied down so that their bottoms are at the same height as the frame members. Open backs and arms have seat springs that are tied only as high above the seat rail as the rail's thickness. Thus, a 4″-wide rail will have springs that are 4″ above the top of the rail. If you tie them closer than that, the springs will rub against the tying twine and burlap, causing them to wear and eventually break.

All springs must be tied down or they will lose their shape; about the loosest you can tie them is 1½″ above their minimum height. The springs should be positioned in straight rows so that you will not have zigzag ties, and seats that feel wobbly. They should be placed on crossover points in the webbing as often as possible. Keep them 2″ away from the inner edges of any exposed seat rails (like the front) and 1″ from rails that are under the arms and back. Keep them at least 1½″ but no more than 4″ apart so they will not distort.

Upholsterers have somehow managed to confuse the two basic patterns used for tying springs by giving them four different names. Two-way tie and four-way tie are the same set of knots; eight-way tie refers to the same knot patterns. The four-knot tie is sometimes referred to as the

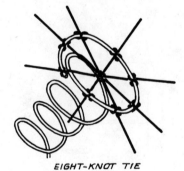

FOUR-KNOT TIE   EIGHT-KNOT TIE

The four-knot and eight-knot ties.

English; and the eight-knot tie is often called the French, diagonal or Union Jack. What all this confusion amounts to is whether you are referring to the number of strings or the number of knots in the tie. For the sake of clarity, the two systems will be referred to here as the *four-knot tie* and the *eight-knot tie,* which means there are either four knots or eight knots applied to the top coil of each spring. When you have completed a four-knot tie, you will have a single strand of twine that runs from the front to the back rail over each spring in the row. The twine is knotted twice to the top of each spring. Then a second strand of twine is stretched between the side rails over the springs and is also tied twice to each spring. An eight-knot tie has the same two basic strands tied to the top coil of each spring, but it also has two diagonal lines, each of which is tied twice to the coils, giving each spring a total of eight knots in its top coil. The four-knot tie produces a resilient cushion to sit on and is used most often for rounded seats. The eight-knot tie is both stiffer and stronger, and so is primarily applied to flat seats.

Tying down springs. You can tie down the twine that holds your springs by tacking it into the frame. Loop an overhand knot over the partially driven tack, tighten it, and then hammer the tack home. A more reliable method, which is almost as quick, is to partially drive (slip-tack) two tacks into the frame, spacing them no farther apart than the diameter of the twine they will hold. Loop the twine around each tack as shown here, and hammer the tacks down.

When you are tying down the coils of a spring, you can simply loop the twine around the coil, but if the twine should ever break, all of the coils it is attached to will come loose. It is safer to tie a simple clove hitch (see page

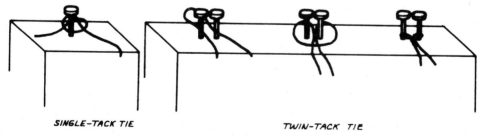

SINGLE-TACK TIE   TWIN-TACK TIE

The preferred method of tying spring twine is to use two tacks.

99) each time the twine crosses a spring coil or another piece of twine. Anytime you are tying the end of a piece of twine to a coil, give it two or three additional half hitches.

When you are tying tight-spring seats that have rounded edges, you will shape the edges by using a system known as return tying. As you bring the twine to the edge coils, do not tie the outermost edge in the top coil; instead, bring the twine down to the outside edge of the second coil from the top. Pull the spring down to height and loop the twine around its tacks. Now return the free end of the twine to the untied outer edge of the upper coil, tie it, then cross the top of the coil and tie off the twine next to the knot on the inside edge of the top coil. Or continue the twine to the inside edge of the next spring and tie it off there. The advantage of return tying is that you can better control the angle of the edge coils and, therefore, more easily vary the shape of the seat—you can even make it absolutely flat.

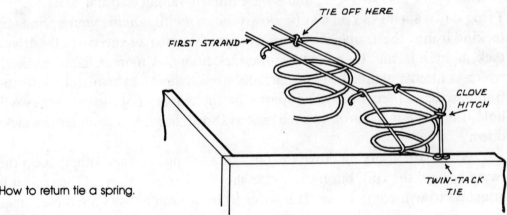

How to return tie a spring.

The process for tying tight-spring seats may sound complicated, but actually comes down to five steps:

1. Begin by placing pairs of tacks centered in front of each row of springs. Drive the tacks partway into the frame (slip-tack them) all the way around the springs. Cut strands of twine that are three times the width of the seat frame, double each strand, and tie them off to the tacks along the back and one side rail.

2. Take one strand from the back and tie it with a half hitch to the outside of the second from the top coil of the edge spring. Then continue the twine to the top coil and tie it. Bring the strand to the second spring, tying it on both

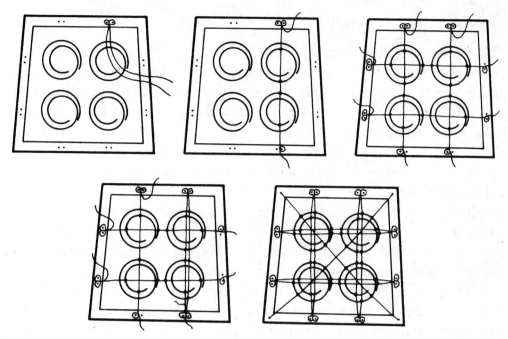

Use an eight-knot tie for tight-spring seats.

edges of the top coil, and continue tying all the springs in the row every time the twine crosses a coil (which means you will have two knots in the top coil of every spring). At the last spring in the row, tie the twine to the inside of the top coil, then drop it down to the outer edge of the second coil. Loop the twine around the tacks and return it to the outside of the top coil. Tie it off.

3. When you have tied all of the springs with one strand from the back to front, tie them with one strand from side to side.

4. The first strands position the springs; the second strands secure them. The second strand, however, is brought up from the tacks to all of the top coils in each spring and tied with a half hitch. The second strand never touches the second highest coil in any spring. When all of the twine is tied off, hammer down the tacks to secure the knots.

5. You can now finish off tying down the springs by adding diagonal lines across the top coils so that they form a cross over the center of each spring. Remember that each time the twine crosses either a coil or another strand of twine, it should be knotted with a clove hitch.

Spring-Edge Seats

The springs in spring-edge seats, which usually support cushions, are tied down in the same manner as for tight-spring seats. However, the springs are different in that they have a piece of wire tied around their top coils, and the top coils of all edge springs are enlarged and bent over the top of the frame rails. When the coils are held flat by the return twine, their outer edges should line up exactly over the outer edge of the rail.

You must shape the springs before they are stitched to the webbing by enlarging the top coil of the spring. You can do this with a knotted spring simply by opening the knot with pliers and forcing it farther down the coil. As the knot is pushed farther down, the top coil will automatically become enlarged and tend to push out on the side opposite the knot. Grip the extended side of the top coil and bend it up until it stands at a 45° angle.

With spring-edge seats, you must also lash a piece of 9-gauge wire around the top coil of each of the edge springs. The wire is bent to conform with the contours of the seat rail, so it may be a simple square or be curved. Number 9-gauge wire is stiff and hard to bend, but there are two ways of shaping it. You can hold the wire against the corner of a hard surface, such as a workbench, or in a vise, and hammer it. You can also insert the wire through two 10″ lengths of pipe and use them as handles to bend the

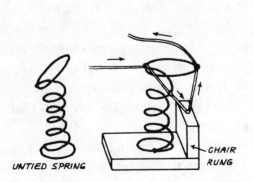

How to tie a tilt-top spring to form a spring-edge seat.

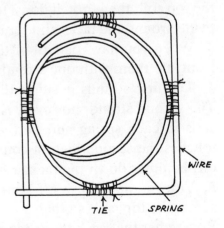

How to lash 9-gauge wire to the top coil of a spring.

wire. Once you have shaped the wire so that it will circle the top coil of the spring, lash it to the top coil at every point it touches the coil. Begin each lash with a clove hitch, then wrap the twine around the wire and coil, crossing and crisscrossing them, and tie off the lashing at the point the ends of the wire separate.

When you stitch the spring to its webbing, place the jutting side of the top coil over the seat rail so that its outer edge is parallel with the outside of the rail. As you return, tie the edge springs; pull the bent-up coil down until it is flat and parallel to the webbing, and comes over the rail.

Spring Backs

The spring coils in seat backs are almost always tied in the same way as seats. The springs themselves are usually KBE and are of a lighter gauge than those used in seats. They are spaced between 2″ and 4″ apart, and normally the four-knot tie is enough to hold them. If you wish to give the back a finer mesh of twine to support the padding, several extra filler ties can be knotted from twine to twine between the springs. The filler ties can either be tied off at the edge wire in spring-edge backs, or brought down to the rail.

When constructing a rounded or contoured back, stitch the springs only to the vertical webbing, with 2″ to 3″ spaces between the top coils in each row. You must tie the springs vertically, since any horizontal ties will get in the way of shaping the contoured back. Consequently, you may have to tie two separate strands, which run parallel through the center of each spring, to give more stability.

Covering the Springs

BURLAP

All springs should be covered so that the stuffing material cannot work its way down between the springs and inhibit their efficiency. Heavy burlap is tacked and sewn over every spring that will reside behind any kind of padding.

You may cut the burlap into wide strips and tack it over the springs, or cut a square that is about 3″ larger along each edge than the area you are covering. Draw the burlap over the springs and tack it at the center of each edge. The burlap is not supposed to receive any pressure from the springs, but is only to protect them from the stuffing, so make it snug but not taut. When the burlap is in position with evenly distributed tension, fold over its edges and tack them to the frame with #3 upholstery tacks spaced every 1½″ along the rails. You may have to cut or slit the burlap and tuck it around the posts to make it curve neatly with the rails.

Using a 2″ or 3″ curved needle and stitching twine, sew the burlap to the top coils of each spring. Sew a lock stitch (a simple overhand knot) at three points in each top coil, then move on to the next spring until all of the springs have been stitched.

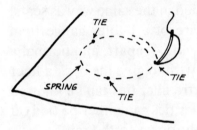

The top coil of each spring should be sewn to the burlap at three points, using a curved needle and lock stitches.

EDGE ROLLS

Edge rolls not only soften the angular lines of furniture, but they also make it more comfortable to sit on. They help keep the stuffing materials in place and also shape the contours of the seating area. You can—and may have to—make your own edge rolling, but you will save time and money if you purchase commercially produced rolls, which range from ¼″ to 1½″ in diameter. Anything larger than 1½″, which you might use to build up uneven portions of a rail, must be handmade.

Commercial edge rolls are usually made of burlap or felt which is rolled over burlap, cotton, rope, paper or almost any other fiber. They are sold by the foot or in long coils. As a rule, use the firmer rolls—they wear better and will not compact as quickly. Select a roll diameter that is equal to the thickness of the padding that will be next to the edge to be softened. The bulk of the roll should rest on the primary surface to be covered. Thus it would sit along the top edge of a seat rail with only a slight overhang beyond

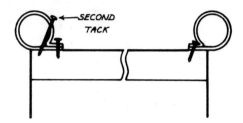

How to tack edge rolls to the furniture frame.

the front of the rail. If both sides of the rail are to be padded, bevel the edge of the rail with a plane so that the edge roll can be tacked at the proper angle. You should, in this instance, use the next larger diameter roll so that when it is compressed by the cover fabric, it still maintains the proper depth with the padding on either side of it.

When tacking an edge roll, first lay it in place and secure it with small tacks driven into the rail. Place the tacks close to the bottom of the roll. Then add longer tacks through the base of the roll itself, angling them into the rail and spacing them about 1½″ apart. When you are going around a corner, cut a triangle out of the back of the roll so that it can be folded against itself to form a mitered angle. If the rolls you are using are loosely stitched and floppy, you can stiffen them along their base by using tacking strips of ½″-wide cardboard laid down on top of the tacking lip.

When you must build up areas beyond 1½″, you can sew more than one roll together. Double each stitch over the roll; pay particular attention to stitching the corners so they will not lose their shape.

Making Edge Rolls

There are any number of ways you can make your own edge rolls. The simplest method is to tack the edge of a strip of burlap along the rail edge that is three or four times wider than the height the roll is to be. Then, starting at the center of each rail and working toward the corners, place the amount of stuffing you need on the burlap. Draw the burlap tightly over your filling and shape it into an even roll. Drive tacks into the overlapping edge of the burlap, placing them next to the bottom row of tacks and making sure that some of them pierce the roll itself.

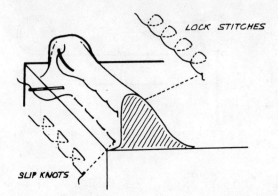

Sewing stitches used to form a triangular edge roll.

Normally, if the roll is less than 1½″ in diameter, it should be round. If it is to be higher than 1½″, form it into a triangle. To produce the triangular shape, sew two rows of compression stitches in the base of the roll. The bottom now is a series of slipknots sewn close to the base. Slightly above the loops, sew a row of lock stitches which draw the roll into its triangular shape. You may wish to add subsequent rows of lock stitches, each a little tighter as you proceed up to the top of the roll. The triangular shape is necessary if you are softening the edges of a platform, padded or edge-spring construction.

You can use an ice pick or heavy needle to push around any lumps that occur inside the roll until you achieve a rounded, even surface. When you reach a corner post, tack the open ends of the burlap to it to prevent the stuffing from working out of the roll.

8

UPHOLSTERY: PADDING AND STUFFING

With burlap smoothly covering the springs and the edge rolls in place and built up to the eventual height of the padding, you can now attach the stuffing to the furniture. There are a variety of paddings and stuffings, which are divided into two categories: 1) coarse, resilient and 2) soft, fine-fibered.

Types of Stuffings

COARSE, RESILIENT STUFFING

The best stuffing is springy, with long individual fibers that can retain their curl. That amounts to a definition of hair, and in the case of furniture stuffing, the hair starts out belonging to horses, cattle or hogs, with the best stuffing coming from the long manes of horses. Hair padding is sold in both loose and rubberized form. The pads are made of rubber-bonded hair, and are between ¾″ and 2½″ thick. They are excellent for padding the majority of a piece of furniture, although loose hair is better for filling in curves or corners.

After hair come its substitutes, which include moss, saran, coco and palm fibers, tampico, sisal, excelsior and tow, all of which are taken from plants or trees. The fibers are held together with a rubber bonding material

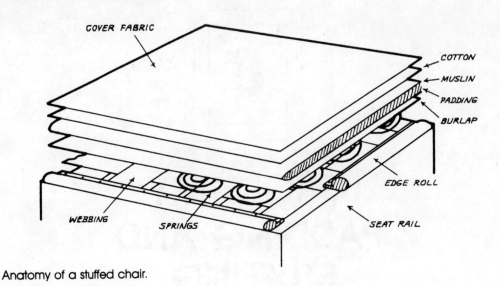

COVER FABRIC

COTTON

MUSLIN

PADDING

BURLAP

EDGE ROLL

WEBBING

SPRINGS

SEAT RAIL

Anatomy of a stuffed chair.

that produces varying degrees of resilience, and therefore varying roles for stuffing furniture.

Moss. Second only to loose hair when it comes to filling corners, curves or shapes. It should always be fluffed and cleaned of lumps and foreign particles before using.

Saran. A synthetic that is also good for slab work, but not curves or shapes.

Coco. Comes from coconut shells and is considered both durable and strong, but is hard to work with. It packs down readily, which makes it useful primarily as an insulator for springs.

Palm. Cheap, clean and durable, palm fibers are usually in inexpensive furniture. Palm is good as a space filler or spring insulator under more resilient stuffings.

Tampico. Resilient, clean, strong and easy to handle, tampico is best as a spring insulator or space filler under hair, moss or foam.

Sisal. Clean and durable, sisal is a good nonresilient understuffing or spring insulator, particularly if you want a firm shape.

Excelsior. This is shredded wood fiber with poor resiliency, so it is quick to mat. Use it only as a spring insulator.

Tow. This comes from flax. It packs into hard layers, making it good for insulating.

SOFT, FINE-FIBERED STUFFINGS

Soft, fine-fibered padding is placed between coarser, springier stuffings and the cover fabric. The major fine-fibered stuffings are cotton, down and feathers, polyester and kapok. Whether it is old or new, fiber stuffing should always be picked apart to break up any hard lumps in the felt, and then fluffed. All foreign particles should be removed. Simply take a handful of fiber and pull it apart until the whole supply has been thoroughly cleaned. Following are descriptions of the basic soft stuffings.

Cotton felt. Cotton actually comes in a full range of toughness and resiliencies, and can have both long or short fibers. You can get it in lumps as well as felted into sheets; the more of the long-fibered stable content, the more resilient the felt. Good staple cotton felt is hard to find these days and has been replaced by substitutes made from quilted batts, polyester mats and resilient sheets of wood fiber. The paper and paper/cotton versions break down rapidly and quickly develop a very low resilience.

Down and feathers. These obviously come from birds, principally water fowl. They provide warmth, softness, lightness and compressibility, making them ideal as the stuffing for pillows, quilts and sleeping bags. Down is rarely used in furniture unless at least 20% of its volume is made up of goose or duck feathers.

Polyester fibers. Soft, clean and durable, polyester holds its shape well and is excellent between foam and pillow casings to provide a puffy look.

Kapok. This is a silky fiber from the kapok tree that does not absorb moisture. It is fairly resilient but in time will pack down under constant pressure and begin to lump and break into powdery pieces.

Foam rubber (polyurethane). This has become popular in recent years because it is easy to work with. It can be purchased in densities of extra soft, soft, medium, firm and extra firm. In many instances one slab of foam rubber can replace all three of the layers normally used in stuffing furniture. It can also be built up with a bottom layer of firm density supporting softer densities.

The Three Layers of Stuffing

Furniture is usually stuffed with three layers of padding which are then encased by a cover fabric. The materials used in each layer are likely to be dictated by cost and availability. If your budget is limited, use the cheapest materials for your first stuffings and save your money for the second and top layers and, of course, the cover fabric.

UNDERSTUFFING

The first layer of stuffing is used specifically to hide any irregularities in the frame and provide a cushion against the feel of the springs; fill in voids; and establish all of the basic shapes in the piece. Always use extremely resilient material such as hair or moss if you are restoring a fine piece of furniture. Less expensive long-haired fibers will, however, do a good job; sisal, tow, palm or tampico actually level and insulate springs better than hair since they compact into firm mats rather quickly.

The first layer is always tacked, stitched, glued or even encased in burlap to prevent its shifting, and it is always retained by the edge rolls. Without exception, the understuffing is made level with the top of the edge rolls and built up in thin layers to shape all of the contours of the finished stuffing.

When the fiber has been picked and fluffed, distribute it over the burlap in a thin, even layer. Overlap each handful and then press it into the preceding material until you have built up the shapes you want. Continue building the fibers in thin layers until they are level with or slightly overlap the edge rolls. Make sure there are no hard or soft, high or low spots anywhere in the padding.

If the stuffing has been laid on a solid base, you can probe down about three-quarters of its depth and then drive tacks through the rest of it. If the stuffing is on top of burlap or webbing, stitch it. Begin sewing either at the

LOOSE SPIRAL
STITCH PATTERN

Stuffing should be tacked or loosely sewn to keep it from shifting. Stitch in a spiral pattern that conforms to the shape of the seat.

center or in any corner, and spiral your stitches either into the center or out to the edges. Start with a short stitch and tie a slipknot in the sewing twine. From then on, use 2″- or 3″-long stitches across the top of the stuffing, and stitches no more than ¾″ long under the burlap or webbing.

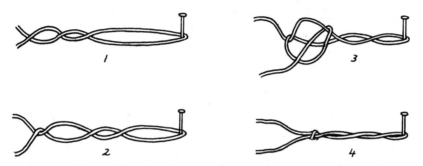

How to tie a slipknot: hold both pieces of twine in one hand and twist them, then loop the knot and draw it tight.

SECOND LAYER

Hair, moss, rubberized fibers and foam are used in the second layer to provide most of the resiliency in the finished piece. In fine furniture, it is the second layer of padding that makes up the bulk of the stuffing. If you have chosen foam it can be used not only for this layer, but for the layers above and below it; in some instances (e.g., a platform seat with loose cushions) there is no need for any stuffing between the first layer and top padding.

Loose hair or moss must be built up two or three times higher than it will be when you compress it. Keep building it on top of the first layer of padding; push down on it with the palm of your hand. When you can no longer feel the first stuffing, the second layer is deep enough.

The second layer of padding is laid in place the same way as the first—in handfuls of thin layers that gradually build up to the desired height. When you get to the right height, keep going in the center of the seat until it is "crowned." Second-layer padding is soft and resilient. The moment you start fastening cover material over it, it will compress; if you are covering a perfectly flat surface made of uncompressed fibers and do not give it a crown, you will wind up with a hollow in the center of the seat.

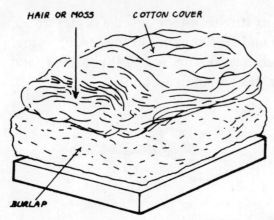

HAIR OR MOSS   COTTON COVER

BURLAP

Loose hair or moss must be built up to about three times its compressed height.

You do not have to stitch the second layer, but it helps, particularly if the undersurface is severely curved. Use stitching twine and a curved needle to loosely stitch the two layers together to keep the stuffing from slipping. You can also stitch a muslin casing over the second stuffing to help compress it into its final shape.

TOP PADDING

The top padding is intended to smooth out any lumps or indentations in the lower stuffings and prevent any coarse particles from poking through to the cover fabric.

Felted cotton, foam, cotton felt substitutes, polyester fibers, rayon and kapok often comprise the top padding. They are sometimes used individually in places where you are interested only in a thin, uniform appearance, such as the insides and outsides of arms or the outsides of backs. With a padded seat, you can lay a series of increasingly larger layers of top padding on top of each other (like an upside-down pyramid) so that the largest pad is draped on top to present a smooth surface for the cover.

Top padding should hang over small edge rolls on any pad, tight-spring seats, backs or round seats. With spring-edge seats, you have to fill in the space between the bottom of the edge roll and the top of the rail with a layer or two of top padding, then lay a single layer over the entire top to give it a smooth, curved surface.

Muslin Covers

Lots of people have stopped using muslin covers because they take time and cost money. Muslin is only a sheet of cotton, and you can skip it as a stage in your reupholstering, but—it will compress the stuffing to the right density and shape. It takes most of the pressure off the cover fabric. It is a kind of dry run for putting the cover on, and as such it represents your last chance to make mistakes. From the muslin on, every error will show.

Muslin is a necessity if you are using a delicate fabric such as velvet or silk as the top cover. The muslin protects the underside of the fabric from chafing against the coarser second layer of stuffing and loosening the fabric's pile.

Used as a dry run, muslin lets you see all the defects in your padding so far and and gives you a chance to correct them. After you have put it over the padding, get out your stuffing rods and regulators. Stuffing rods are steel bars or strips of ⅛″-thick wood (a yardstick is ideal). Regulators are flat ended or blunt ended, like dulled ice picks. Of the two shapes, the flat-ended ones are more useful for pushing around pieces of material. Poke the rods and regulators through the muslin to push around or break up lumps of padding and work the stuffing into hard-to-reach corners.

Determine what size to cut your muslin by placing a tape measure over the stuffing and pulling it down to the rails so that the padding is compressed to its final height. Measure from front to back and from side to side, then add 4″ to each dimension and cut the muslin. Slip-tack the muslin at the

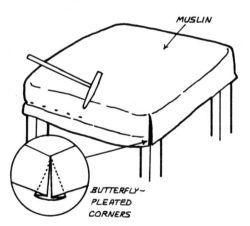

Slip-tack muslin at the center of each side and keep it taut as you tack toward the corners.

MUSLIN

BUTTERFLY-
PLEATED
CORNERS

center point of each rail, then smooth it out, keeping it taut as you begin tacking toward the corners. Rather than doing one side at a time, you will find it easier to put one or two tacks in one side, then work on the opposite rail. Grip the muslin a few inches from the last tack and pull it taut, then tack it. Pleat each corner neatly, using a simple butterfly pleat at sharp corners and a series of small, flat pleats when going around curves.

When your tacking is finished, shine a strong light on the padding and inspect the muslin for pulls, dips, lumps, wrinkles and any other fault. Repair all of the imperfections you find by removing the necessary tacks and repositioning them, or by using your stuffing regulators. Only when you have achieved a perfectly smooth surface should the slip tacks be driven home.

Tips About Foam Rubber

Foam rubber can be used in any number of ways to pad furniture, and offers the advantage of not demanding the precision that fiber materials do. It is not unusual to use foam rubber by itself, either as a single layer of padding or as a firm, then a medium and finally a soft layer set on top of each other. You can also lay a polyester or a cotton felt padding over the foam to reduce the elastic tautness that often occurs in the fabrics used to cover foam. Foam is useful on arms and backs, particularly in recessed areas that need to be built up.

You can cut foam rubber with a serrated knife, a stationary band saw or a foam cutter. The cutting tool that is probably most efficient is an electric carving knife. Only the band saw, electric knife and foam cutter will cut all the way through foam that is more than 2″ thick. You must repeatedly draw a sharp, serrated blade across the surface, cutting only as deep as you can go without causing the foam to compress. Foam bulges, compresses and clings to whatever tool is cutting it. To cut curves for a crowned effect, it is usually better to use scissors moistened with a dry silicone lubricant or water. You will undoubtedly leave uneven edges in the foam no matter how you cut it, but they can be buffed smooth with a belt or disk sander, using #80 or #120 granite or aluminum oxide paper.

Foam adhesives are invaluable when working with padding, and you should use the best one you can find. The cheaper types tend to create a hard

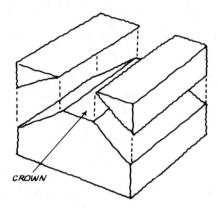

Foam can be crowned by gluing successively smaller layers on top of each other, or by cutting triangles off the edges of the slab.

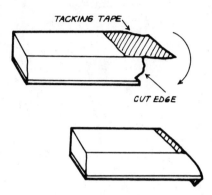

Tacking tape is useful for shaping foam edges. Glue the tape to the top of the edge, then draw the tape down and tack it.

joint that eventually crumbles, whereas the joint should remain as soft as the material around it.

Tacking tape is also useful for holding foam in place, as well as for shaping edges. You can buy it in widths ranging from 2″ to 6″. They are either fully covered with adhesive on one side or have only a strip of adhesive along one edge.

Apply adhesive to all foam surfaces to be joined and allow it to become tacky, then press the dry tacking tape to one of the surfaces. Gently position the gluing surfaces, then press them together. Be exact about your positioning; the pieces will be hard to separate once they have come together. Although you can handle foam-to-foam joints 10 minutes after gluing, give them several hours to set before putting any stress on them, particularly if you have glued the foam to wood or metal. Dust all surfaces around any glued joint with talcum powder (any type will do) to absorb the excess adhesive.

Channeling

Channeling and tufting (see pages 140–142) change the look of furniture, and are useful ways of making fabric conform to curved inner surfaces. Channeling, which is also known as fluting and shell backing, is essentially a

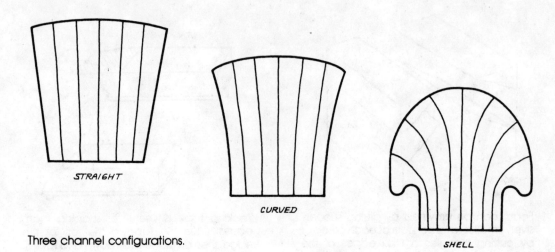

STRAIGHT

CURVED

SHELL

Three channel configurations.

technique of stuffing pipes (or channels) to give a ribbed effect, and it is usually applied to the backs of chairs. The channels can be curved, straight or fanned out to produce a shell effect, and the width of each channel can be anywhere from 1″ to 8″ or so. The width used, as well as the rest of the design, depend largely on the style of the piece being upholstered and your personal taste. As a general rule, however, all the channels in a given piece should be pretty much the same width, size and shape, and have the same density of stuffing.

Channels must be supported on a burlap base, never on loose stuffing. You can prepare the base as you would any flat or curved surface. If you decide on an even number of channels, there will be a depression (really a seam) down the center of the surface to be covered. If there is an odd number of channels, the center channel should be positioned directly over the centerline.

To determine the width of each channel, measure the width of both the top and bottom edges of the surface to be covered. If the back fans out at the top and the channels are to be curved, be very careful that each panel is equal in width and has identical curves—it will be very obvious if there is any size variation. The channels should be at least 2″ thick at their centers, but they can taper or vary if you want to achieve different effects. You can, for example, straighten a tilted chair back merely by thickening the bottom and flattening the tops of the channels.

When you have determined the dimensions of your channels, make an exact pattern of their shape out of paper, allowing 1″ for the seam on either side and 3″ at each end. A single pattern can be used for all of your channels if they are identical; the patterns are useful not only when you are cutting muslin for the channels themselves, but for the cover fabric as well. Also measure and then chalk-mark exactly where the seams will fall on the furniture surface. Having done all this, you can now make your channels.

Use your paper pattern for cutting each piece of muslin, allowing for 1″ seams. Machine-sew the pieces to a base piece of muslin that will fit against the top padding of the chair. Align the muslin and channels by laying the center seam along its corresponding chalk mark on the chair. Slip-tack the bottom of the seam with one tack, then stretch the channel and slip-tack it to the top rail with a single tack. Lock-stitch the first seam to the supporting surface or, if you are working over wood, put cardboard tacking strips over the seam allowances. When the center channel is in position, stuff it with hair, moss, foam or whatever padding you have elected to use. Then repeat the process with each of the channels until they are all in place and properly stuffed. Outside channels may require some extra care; they will be very conspicuous if they are not uniform in size and shape.

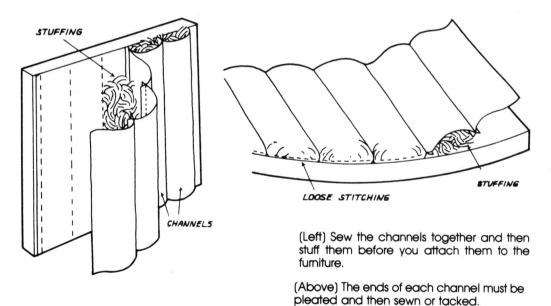

STUFFING

CHANNELS

LOOSE STITCHING

STUFFING

(Left) Sew the channels together and then stuff them before you attach them to the furniture.

(Above) The ends of each channel must be pleated and then sewn or tacked.

When you are finished, check your work and readjust any stuffing with your regulator until the channels are as uniform as possible. Only then should you tack the bottoms of the channels. Be sure the top of the channels, where they wrap over the back of the seat, are properly stuffed. Slip-tack the top of each channel to the top rail, then rip out enough of the seams between channels to make pleats as the muslin crosses over the top rail.

Pleats should always fall in the channel seams. Normally, upholsterers pleat a little less than one-quarter of the excess muslin width in the middle of the channel, and form a covering pleat across its edges. Form your pleats and slip-tack them. Make whatever adjustments are necessary to achieve a uniform appearance, drive your tacks home and trim off any excess muslin. Use the smallest tacks that will hold the muslin in place.

Tufting

Tufting is the business of creating a pattern of mounds in an upholstered surface. Usually the pattern is diamond-shaped, held with buttons tied tightly to the backing to hold the tuft in place. The diamond pattern presents a variety of visual effects if you change its shape, width, length and thickness. Tufts can be filled with cotton, felt, polyester or foam.

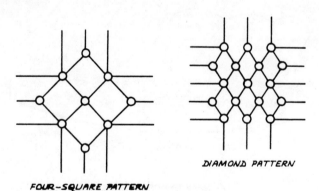

FOUR-SQUARE PATTERN

DIAMOND PATTERN

Two tufting patterns. The designs that can be worked out using the basic diamond shape are almost infinite.

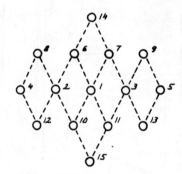

The button positions for a diamond pattern. The numbers refer to the order in which the position is tightened.

TUFTING WITH FIBER

Begin by making a paper pattern of the tuft shape and then trace it in chalk on the surface to be tufted. Draw a centerline down the middle of the surface with chalk, and arrange your design around it as symmetrically as possible. The four corners of each diamond will have buttons in them, and the button points should be marked along with the diagonal pleat lines that extend from button to button. When you have marked the button positions on the surface, poke a needle through them and mark the backing with chalk or, if you are working against wood, drill ¼" holes.

How much fabric you cut is determined by measuring the largest tuft horizontally and vertically from button to button, then multiplying the two dimensions by the number of tufts you plan to have. Add the distance from the outside tufts to the edge of the piece, plus 6" for every 1½" of stuffing thickness.

Whatever surface you are tufting should be stuffed in the usual manner with three layers of padding, except that the top layer should be made of resilient hair, moss or foam that is thick enough to make the desired tufts. For each button, cut a length of twine approximately 3' long. Loop the twine down through the stuffing, around the backing and out through the surface again; the stitch should be ¼" across the back of the button point. Leave equal lengths of twine on each side of the hole, and twist the two strands together so they will not come apart. Now build up the area of the tuft around each buttonhole, always keeping the twine taut as you go. When the stuffing is high enough, carefully separate the twine with your finger or a regulator, and push all of the stuffing out from between the strands. As you lay the muslin over the button points, poke the strands of twine through it, leaving ¼" of space between them. You will find that using a crochet hook is easier than a needle.

Wherever a button is positioned, tie a length of twine to the backing and bring it up through the muslin with the paired button twine. You don't have to do anything with this channel twine for the moment except let about ½" of it hang out of the muslin.

When the muslin is in place, slipknot each pair of button twine strands, and draw the muslin against the stuffing. Do *not* pull the muslin down against the backing. Start tying the button twine at or near the center and work out toward the edges.

The stuffing must be drawn down to the backing material so that it is even. To do this, tighten the slipknots at each button point only a little at a time until all of the knots have grounded against the backing material. You may have to use your regulator to keep the stuffing between buttons from shifting or sagging; this should be done before the knots are tied off with an overhand knot. When the knots are tied, cut off any excess twine and pleat the material between button points by smoothing down the folds with the flat end of your regulator.

Now pull the channel twines taut against the muslin along the edges of each channel (between the button points). Push the stuffing away from the twine, then tack the free end of the twine at the same place along the rails as the edge of the muslin; pleat the muslin over the twine.

TUFTING WITH FOAM

Foam is actually simpler to tuft than fibers. Cut a slab of foam that is thick enough to allow for the tufting and mark the button positions. Cement or tack the foam to its supporting surface, then punch 1″-deep holes through it at each button point. Tie the channel and tufting twine in the holes, thread the strands through the muslin cover, then tighten the twine. If you want clearly defined tufting and channel lines, use a serrated knife to slice about two-thirds of the way through the foam between the buttons and along the channels before you put on the muslin. The muslin will pull the edges of your cuts into sharply delineated valleys.

9

UPHOLSTERY: COVERING UP

The fabrics used as final covers in upholstering are categorized according to their weight, and are sold in widths of 36″, 48″, 50″ or 54″ and any number of lengths. The heaviest group includes chenille, crewel, embroidery, frieze, matelassé, plush, needlepoint, quilting, tapestry, tweed, velour and velvet. All of these are capable of holding tuft and channel pleats better than lighter materials. They are all considered easy to work with, although you may encounter some problems if you are sewing two pieces of heavy fabric together on a home sewing machine.

The medium-weight fabrics are linen, monk's cloth, sailcloth, damask, corduroy, brocatelle, satin and ticking, all of which are nearly as easy to work with as the heavyweight group. The medium weights will create less bulky corner pleats, but tuft and channel pleats made with medium-weight materials are not so well defined.

Lightweight upholstery fabrics take in silk, sateen, muslin, moire, denim, chintz and broadcloth. The big problem with the lightweights is that they tend to rip during installation and almost never make a good-looking pleat.

When you choose a cover fabric, you not only have the weight of the material to consider, but its pattern, color and texture as well. You must also take into account the design of the furniture and the look you want it to have, which means you also have to determine whether you will use trim, welt, brush or boucle edgings, gimp, or skirts and their smaller version, ruching. By the time you are ready to put on your final fabric, you have already devoted a considerable amount of time, effort and expense. It pays to sit down and think out every detail of the finished piece.

The Preliminaries

MEASURING

Don't trust the original pieces of cover material. They have probably stretched. They are, of course, the best guide you have as far as shapes and the placement of seams and tacks are concerned, but you still have to measure everything.

For purposes of clarity, *length* refers to the direction of lengthwise warp threads in the cloth. As a rule, length is also the top-to-bottom pattern or grain of the fabric. *Width* is at right angles to the length, that is, the narrower dimension (36″ to 54″) of the cloth.

When you cut fabric, always measure its width first, since this is the more limiting of the two dimensions and controls whether or not you will have to piece together the material. All measurements should be made from attaching point to attaching point, whether that will be tacks or stitching. Make as accurate a set of dimensions for each piece as you can, adding 1″ for each seam and 3″ for handling. Mark each attaching point with an S (for seam) or a T (for tacking) and also identify the piece with a code like the one shown here.

CODE FOR IDENTIFYING COVER PIECES

Mark each cover piece on its back with one of the following letters. When marking an outside piece also include the letter **O** (for outside). If you are cutting fabric for a welt or border, mark its position as well as what it is. Thus, a piece of fabric for the welt on the outside of an arm would be marked **A** (arm) **O** (outside) **Wt** (welt), and written **AO-Wt**.

A	Arm (inside)	**Bx**	Boxing	**P**	Panel	**Sk**	Skirt
B	Back (inside)	**C**	Cushion		(or facing)	**St**	Stretcher
Ba	Banding		(or pillow)	**R**	Ruching	**W**	Wing (inside)
Br	Border	**O**	Outside	**S**	Seat	**Wt**	Welt

Every piece, no matter what its ultimate shape, is measured as if it were a rectangle. It goes without saying that a flexible tape measure that can bend over the contours of your stuffing is more accurate than a rigid wooden yardstick.

Skirts and ruching strips are measured with their narrow dimension as the length and the long dimension as the width. No matter which of the three types of pleats you are making (see diagram), allow 1″ for piecing seams and 1″ for closing seams. With a normal skirt, the length is figured from the bottom rail to the floor, plus 3″ for the hem, top tacking and handling, which allows you to tack the skirt ¾″ above the bottom edge of the seat rails. If you are upholstering a ruffled boudoir chair, the length of the ruch strip that

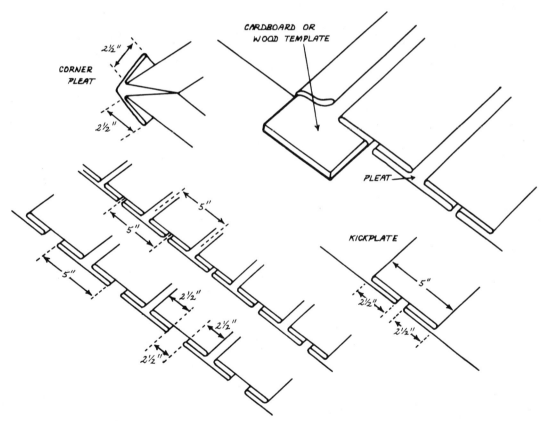

The dimensions for kick, full box and open box pleats. When shaping a pleat, slide a piece of cardboard between the folds of the fabric before you stitch them so that each pleat will be identical.

makes up the ruffle must be twice the amount of ruching that will be seen, plus 2″ for stitching and handling. The width, of course, depends on which kind of pleat you are using and how long an edge it will cover.

LAYING OUT COVERS

Having made reasonably accurate measurements and written them down on rough sketches, you can now make a cutting layout and pattern. The layout should be full size; you may find it easier to tape several pieces of graph paper together and use its squares as guides. When each piece has been drawn and cut out, lay the pattern on the right side of the fabric and trace it with chalk. Cut the fabric along your chalk lines, mark its top edge and identify the piece on its back.

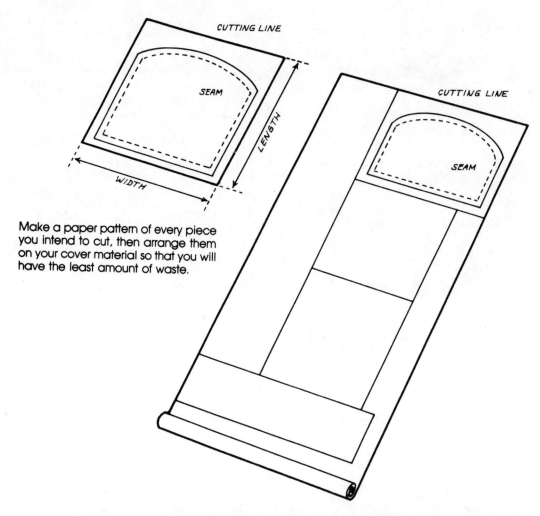

Make a paper pattern of every piece you intend to cut, then arrange them on your cover material so that you will have the least amount of waste.

Sewing Covers

With the exception of cushions, most final covers are hand sewn, usually with blind stitching, although at times a backstitch or running, overhand or tack stitches are called for. Straight stitching with a machine is used on welting and edge finishing as well as for such decorative techniques as trapunto, false channeling and quilting. Following are the seams commonly used for furniture covers.

Flat seams. These are made by placing the two edges of the material over each other and stitching approximately 1″ inside the edges. The seam allowance is then opened and pressed flat.

French seams. Place the edges together with the wrong sides facing out and stitch them ¼″ beyond the seam line. Trim the seam allowance to ⅛″ and press the seam open. Fold the material back over the seam allowances so that the wrong sides face each other, and stitch along the seam line. Spread the material and press the seam allowance to one side.

Lap seams. Place the edges of the material together so they are right side up and overlap each other by about an inch. Then stitch them with one or more rows.

Trim

THREE KINDS OF WELT

Welt is a piece of cord encased in cover fabric and is an excellent medium for hiding the irregularities of hand stitches. There are three kinds of welt: single, self and double, all of which you can make yourself.

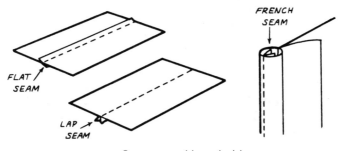

Seams used in upholstery.

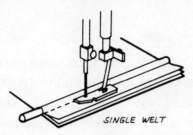
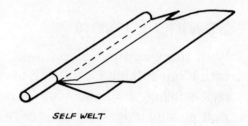

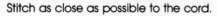

Stitch as close as possible to the cord.

Single Welt

The width of the encasing cover fabric should be three times the diameter of the cord, plus 2″. Lay the cord along the centerline of the strip, fold the fabric over it and stitch as close as you can to the cord, using a zipper foot on your sewing machine.

If you are machine-stitching the welt to a seam, lay the welt between the two pieces of cover fabric with the cord just inside the seam line, then stitch as close to the cord as you can. If the seam is to be blind-stitched, sew the welt to whichever piece will be most visible so that the blind stitch ends up under the welt.

Self Welt

If you have two pieces of fabric to be sewn together and encase the cord in one of the fabric edges, you have a self welt. Add three times the diameter of the cord to the 1″ seam allowance. Place the cord against the underside of the seam line, then fold the cloth over it so that it extends 1″ past the cord. Lay the two fabric edges right side up so that their seam edges are together with the cord sandwiched between them. Stitch as close to the cord as you can.

Double Welt

You can buy double-welt filler that looks like a capital B or use two cords to make a double welt. The double welt is normally gimp-tacked or glued over tacking lines on exposed wood edges. If you are using two cords, cut the welt strip to a width of seven times the diameter of the cord, plus 2″. Put one cord

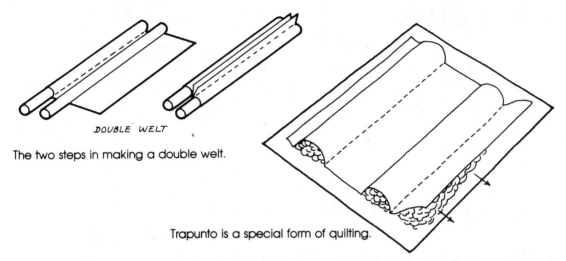

DOUBLE WELT

The two steps in making a double welt.

Trapunto is a special form of quilting.

down the middle of the strip, fold the fabric over it, and stitch it close to the cord. If the welt is to be sewn over a seam, place the second cord next to that row of stitches, bring the other edge of the fabric over the cord and sew it along its outside edge. If the welt is to be glued or tacked to exposed wood, stitch between the cords and trim off any excess material.

QUILTING

The traditional stuffing in quilting is cotton, but rubber, polyester and foam are also popular. Pile stuffing on a thin muslin or cambric backing and cover it with the cover fabric, then machine stitch it. You can use different colored threads and stitch any design you fancy, using a standard quilting attachment on your sewing machine.

TRAPUNTO

A specialized form of quilting used as a decorative feature, trapunto is a raised band of quilting held between rows of stitches. At the point you have completed sewing the cover, place the area to be decorated face down on a table and mark the trapunto design in the center of the piece. Cut a strip of muslin 2″ wider than the space between where the stitches will be, and fill the space with strips of cotton or foam. Pin together the stuffing, muslin and cover, then stitch along the design lines. Remove any excess stuffing and trim the muslin close to the stitch lines.

FALSE CHANNELING

You can make false channels by stitching parallel rows through the cover to the muslin. A layer of soft foam or polyester 1½″ or 2″ thick should be placed between the underside of the cover fabric and the muslin backing. Machine-sew with medium-length stitches to create the depressions between the channels. The foam under the stitches will be compressed, producing a rounded channel between them. For sharper edges, slice the foam from its top to within ¼″ of the muslin side, then stitch through the cuts.

Putting on the Cover

Assuming that muslin has been put over the three layers of padding, you have already used all the basic techniques needed to install a final cover. The only difference is that with muslin, you could make mistakes and correct them with relative ease. With a cover fabric, work very carefully to produce smooth surfaces and be certain that the padding has no lumps or voids in it. Most cover materials will show the marks of a regulator or anything else you

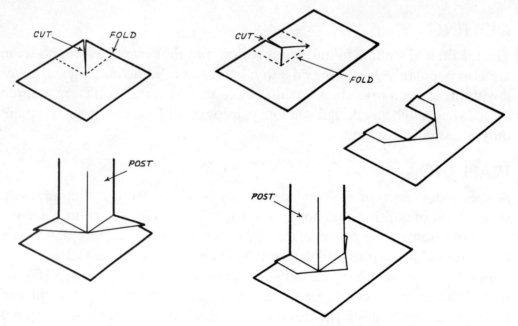

Where to cut fabric to fit it around two or three sides of an obstruction.

poke through it, so you can use a regulator only by going under the cloth. Also be careful to keep your hands and working surfaces clean of oil, ink or glue, all of which will indelibly stain the fabric.

The order in which pieces are put on furniture can vary, but in general the seat is done first, then the inside arms, inside wings, inside back, outside arms, outside wings and lastly the outside back.

FITTING AROUND CORNERS AND POSTS

Anytime you approach a corner, arm, stump or back post, slip-tack the fabric in the center of each side a few inches from the obstruction, and smooth the fabric up to the frame. Mark where the fabric touches the frame, then cut the fabric as shown. Make your cuts just far enough beyond the frame position so that the edges can be folded under.

ANCHORING AND HIDING EDGES

The major task in attaching cover fabric, once it has been smoothed, is to anchor the fabric firmly to the frame, without leaving any visible fabric edges. To this end, you have recourse to tacking strips, banding, borders, welts and panels.

Banding

The fronts of spring-edge and platform seats usually have banding made from a separate strip of material that is wrapped around the seat edge. The strip is attached to the top edge of the seat under a single or self welt. You can line up the welt with the edge wire on the springs and turn down the seam allowance, then pin the welt seam allowance in place with skewer pins. Stick the pins through the banding welt seam, not the cover, and stitch the banding to the muslin covering the seat with 1″ running stitches. Lay cotton felt, polyester or foam under the banding to within ½″ of wherever you will tack the bottom of the banding to the face of the bottom rail. Pull the banding over the padding, smooth it, and tack it ½″ below where the border will be placed. If there is to be no border, wrap the bottom edge under the rail and tack it there.

Borders

These are really bandings that are completely on framing members, so they are tacked along both edges. They can be used along the bottom edge of banding on rail faces, on arms and back posts, and across the top of back rails; you can also sew a welt over their edges.

The top edge of the border is blind-tacked, and then polyester, cotton felt or foam is inserted under the border. The fabric is then pulled smoothly over the stuffing and slip-tacked. Push a regulator under (not through) the border to adjust the stuffing, then drive home your tacks.

Panels

You can stuff a panel after it is in place or before it is installed. Overlay panels are made of thin plywood, plastic or metal, and are covered before they are attached to the face of an arm stump or back post. Metal and plastic are harder to handle than a piece of ½″ or ¾″ plywood, unless you have the equipment to shape them properly. Assuming you choose wood, cut it to fit whatever shape it is covering and pad it with a thin layer of cotton felt or

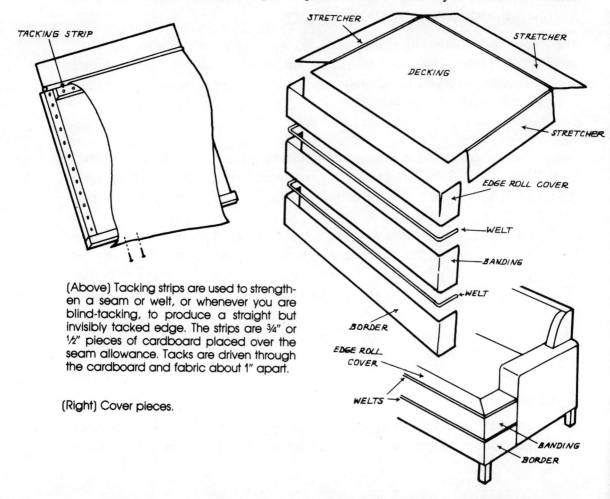

(Above) Tacking strips are used to strengthen a seam or welt, or whenever you are blind-tacking, to produce a straight but invisibly tacked edge. The strips are ¾″ or ½″ pieces of cardboard placed over the seam allowance. Tacks are driven through the cardboard and fabric about 1″ apart.

(Right) Cover pieces.

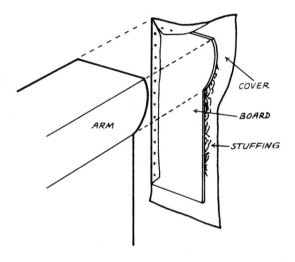

Panels can be stuffed and covered before they are installed.

COVER

BOARD

ARM

STUFFING

foam. Cut the cover fabric 2″ larger all around than the panel. Wrap it over the stuffing and around the panel, and tack it to the back.

To attach the panel, spread the threads of the cover fabric with your regulator and drive finishing nails through the panel and into the furniture. Use a nailset to get the head of the nails through the fabric, then push the threads back over the nail holes with your regulator.

Alternatively, you can make a paper pattern of the panel and cut your cover fabric with a 1″ allowance all around. Slip-tack one side of the shape and insert your stuffing, then tack down the fabric using the nearly invisible gimp tape or decorative upholstery tacks.

SEATS

Anytime a cover extends onto exposed wood, put padding under it as far as the tacking point. Turn under the fabric edge and slip-tack it, then regulate the stuffing, smooth the cover and drive home the tacks. The only time you do not put stuffing between the rail and the cover is when the material is tacked to the underside of the rail. If that is what you are doing, pad only as far as the bottom corner of the seat rail. Normally, if the edges of a seat are enclosed by arms or a back, the cover is tacked to the top of the seat rails. The front rail of the seat can have banding and/or borders.

INSIDE ARMS

Arms can be open, with upholstered arm rests, or fully upholstered with no open spaces between the seat and the arms.

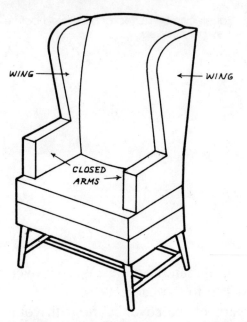

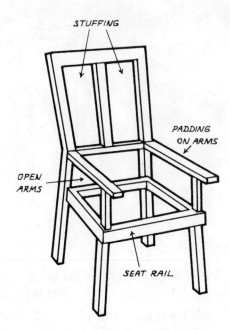

Chairs can be open armed or fully upholstered.

Open Arms

Many arms have a fully covered arm rest, others only a small padded area along the top of the rest. The padding is covered with muslin and a piece of cotton felt is fitted over the muslin before the upholstery is put on. The cotton should stop approximately ¼" from the tacking point. Center the cover material over the cotton and slip-tack it on all four sides. Then smooth it and finish tacking it. If pleats are required, make several very small ones rather than a few large ones since you are working with a relatively small area.

If the cover is to end behind the back post, pull the fabric toward the post as you are tacking it, then cut it and wrap it around the post. You can make the arms look thinner by eliminating the extra cotton felt on their sides, but they will be less comfortable to lean against. It is also wise to slip-tack both arms and then look at them to be sure they appear identical before you drive your tacks home.

Fully Covered Arms

The material over fully covered arms can be attached in several sections or as a unit. Whether there is padding on the arm or not, tack a piece of cotton felt over the arm and on both its sides, ending up about ¼" inside the tacking points on the rails. Unless it is to extend a considerable distance beyond the corner, do not bring the cotton around any edges lest it cause ripples and pull marks. Stop the cotton just beyond any area that will be covered by the seat or back fabric. Position your cover material over the cotton and slip-tack it at the center of its top and bottom edges. The bottom edge of the material is tacked to the top of the seat rail or to the seat cover. If the cover is to go around the back corner post, pull the material toward the back as you smooth it. You can, of course, finish tacking for gimp or double welt trim.

The face of an arm stump that is to be covered by a panel requires that you pleat the cover fabric around the front edge of the stump and then tack the pleats. When the arm is finished, it can be trimmed with banding, borders or a skirt.

INSIDE WINGS

Wing covers can be extensions of the back of the arm covers or they can be covered separately, depending on your preference and the construction of the piece being finished. If you are covering the wings separately, slip-tack or pin the fabric at the center of each edge and turn in the bottom edge where it joins the arm, then blind-stitch it to the arm cover. You may have to slit and pleat it to make the material fit smoothly. Then draw the cover tightly over the wing and tack it to the wing post. Wings are a little tricky because of their curves, but you can add welting or borders to hide any irregularities in the seams.

INSIDE BACKS

You need to put a pad of cotton felt over the burlap on inside backs before the cover material is attached. The cotton should never overlay the frame, but rather end about ½" from the tacking points.

Open Backs

These are backs that have a space between the seat and back frame, so the back padding is essentially an unconnected section of the furniture which is finished on all edges. If the back is fully covered, the cover is normally pulled around the back posts and rails, then tacked to the inside edges of the frame; however, if the framing members are wide enough, the cover is tacked ¾″ inside their outside edges. If there is to be any banding or border, tack the cover just far enough so it will be covered. You do not have to fold the edges over when tacking a back cover, but you may have to make an occasional seam to get rid of wrinkles. If you must slit the fabric, blind-stitch it when you are closing the material. If the back is crowned, tack the top and bottom edges first; for scooped backs, tack the sides first to establish the curve before you stretch the fabric from top to bottom. If the back touches fully padded chair arms, fold the back cover under and pull it tight before tacking it to the insides of the back posts.

Closed Backs

A fully covered back continues to below the level of the seat, where it hides the back edge of the seat. Most fully covered backs have three sections—the back and a separate piece for each arm. Pin the back piece in place and mark the seam location along the front edge of the arm posts from the arm to the seat rails. Pin the arm pieces in place and then remove all three pieces and sew them with either welted or French seams.

When you slip-tack the pieces in place, work from the center of the back out to the arms as you smooth and tighten the material. Pull the fabric

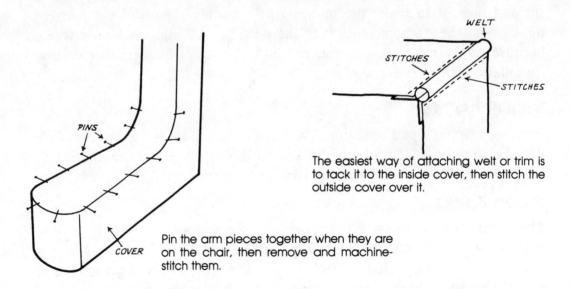

The easiest way of attaching welt or trim is to tack it to the inside cover, then stitch the outside cover over it.

Pin the arm pieces together when they are on the chair, then remove and machine-stitch them.

around the arm posts and tack them to the inside edge of the frame. If you use welting, edging or ruching, it must be placed between the inside and outside covers, but it can be sewn to either cover before it is installed. It is simpler if you tack trim over the edge of the inside cover and then stitch on the outside cover. If you are installing welt, use a cardboard strip to tack it over the inside cover edges, and then blind-stitch the back cover.

CHANNELS

As you place the cover material over a channeled back, work the material into each of the depressions between the channels and slip-tack the bottom of each channel to the top of the seat rail. You may have to open an inch or two of the seams holding the channel twine in order to get the fabric properly taut. Smooth the cover upward, and slip-tack it to the top rail at the center of each channel. You will have to pleat and tack the top edges of the channels in the same manner as the muslin casing was pleated (see pages 135–136).

TUFTS

Before you cover tufting, check it to be sure each of the diamonds is the proper size and shape. Then cut the cover material and mark the tuft location on its underside. Tear pieces of cotton felt that are a little larger than each tuft and center the pads over the tufts. Cut or tear a 1″-diameter hole at each of the button points, and position the cover fabric over the cotton padding.

Buttons

Tie a 2′ or 3′ length of twine to the button loop so that the twine ends are equal, then thread both ends through a needle. Pull the twine through the cover, the tufting, its backing and the webbing. Place a ball of cotton against the webbing between the two twine ends, and pull the button as tightly as you wish; then tie off the twine with a square knot. If you are attaching the buttons to wood, bring the twine through the ¼″ hole drilled through the backing and tie it around slip tacks placed 1″ from the edge of the hole; tighten the button, tie it off and hammer down the tacks.

Continue tying buttons at the corner of each tuft, working from the center tufts out toward the edges. Whenever necessary, use a regulator shoved under (not through) the fabric to adjust the cotton padding.

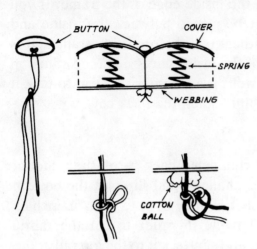

How to tie, sew and tighten tufting buttons.

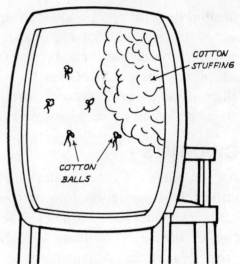

Small voids in the outside of furniture can be filled with lumps of cotton. Large spaces must be filled with wood, cardboard or webbing, which is then padded.

OUTSIDE SURFACES

Before you entirely close the piece of furniture, sit on it. Make sure that all of the stuffing is even and comfortable, and there are no wrinkles showing anywhere. This is your last chance to correct any slackness or eliminate any visible errors. When you are sure that all the front covers are perfectly attached, place a thin pad of cotton felt over the outside webbed or solid surfaces to be covered. If you have large spaces between the frame pieces, they must be filled so that the cover will not be damaged during the furniture's use. Little voids can often be stuffed with loose cotton. Large areas should be given webbing or covered with burlap tacked tightly over the area. You can also nail pieces of lauan or heavy cardboard over large areas. It is best if the wood or cardboard is inserted in rabbets along the inside edges of the frame members, but that may not always be possible. Failing that, tack small blocks of wood about an inch inside the outer edge of the frame members, then nail the backing to the blocks and cover it with cotton felt.

Whenever possible, blind-tack or blind-stitch the top edges of a back cover. If the top edge is curved, you may have to slit the fabric to achieve the proper contours before you tack it. If you are tacking, use a cardboard strip (tackboard) to make the fold line follow the proper configuration. Smooth the cotton padding over the tackboard and pull the cover downward, smoothing and tightening it as you slip-tack it to the underside of the seat rail.

Arms and wings must have the outside edges of their back covers folded under and tacked along their front edges, or you can blind-stitch the edges flush with any edging, welt or ruching that has been installed. If there is a panel to be installed over the front of arms or wings, bring the front edge of the outside cover around the edge and blind-tack it as you did the inside covers.

Back edges are normally brought around the back of posts and tacked. If you want a continuous arm-to-back look, blind-stitch the back to the side covers along the outer edges of the back posts. The outside back covers are put on last. Blind-tack or blind-stitch the top edge as well as the side edges and tack the tightened cover under the seat rails.

After the back covers are installed, put on any panels, gimp or double welt that is intended to cover the outer edges.

FRINGES, SKIRTS AND DUST PANELS

Dust panels are pieces of cambric stretched across the underside of seats and open arms. The cambric is cut 1″ larger than each dimension of the area to be covered. Turn the edges under ¾″ and slip-tack them ¼″ from the outside of the rails. Tighten the cover and tack it in place.

Skirts or fringes are attached last of all and should be blind-stitched to the bottom edge of the cover material. They should hang to within ½″ of the floor.

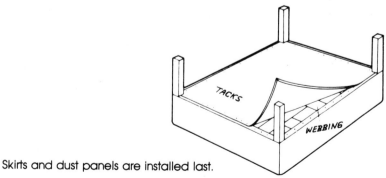

Skirts and dust panels are installed last.

SOFT TOUCHES: CUSHIONS, PILLOWS AND BOLSTERS

Bolsters, pillows and cushions are used with, or in place of, furniture. While they may assume a full measure of sizes, shapes and densities, they are of three basic types: *Fitted seat and back cushions* are built up around springs and can be used on both open-frame and overstuffed furniture. They can have inner springs encased in rubber or foam, which is then covered with down, feathers, cotton or fibers. *Throw pillows* are always small and can be stuffed with just about anything, including foam, polyester, cotton, kapok or feathers. *Unsupported shaped pillows*, or *bolsters*, may be used as backrests or be large enough to put on the floor. They are generally thicker than other types of cushions and are often built up around a core of rubberized fiber or foam.

Fitted Cushions

Cushions made to fit into the exact space of a back or seat must be self-contained units, and therefore their covers should fit smoothly, but your real problem is to make them in the exact size allowed by the seat or back and its arms.

    Don't even think about making fitted cushions until the final cover material is on the chair because if the cushion is more complicated than a simple square, you can easily be fooled by what looks like identical spaces and contours. For example, you might think the arms are both the same size, but they may well have turned out slightly different in thickness, a fact that will affect the cushion's measurements.

The best approach to determining the dimensions of a fitted pillow is to make a pattern of the chair seat or back and then turn it over so that the sides are reversed. If the pattern fits the contours of both the left and right sides of the seat (or back), you can go ahead and use it for the top and bottom covers. But if you discover any variations you will either have to adjust the arms, back and seat to produce identical contours, or make a cushion that is not reversible. There is a small cost advantage to making nonreversible cushions: the bottom can be made of a less expensive fabric than the cover material.

When you are cutting your pattern, add an allowance of 1″ wherever there is to be a seam, plus an additional ¾″ to both the length and width if the pillows are to be extra-full. Presumably you have already allocated rectangles for the cushions in your cover fabric and marked them *cushion top, cushion bottom, cushion boxing* and *cushion welting*. Check your dimensions to be sure each of these rectangles is large enough for the purpose you have in mind, and then cut them out, following the directions below.

CONSTRUCTION

How to Cut Covers

1. Lay the piece of fabric marked *cushion top* right side up on the chair seat and smooth it out.

2. Draw a seam line around the edges of the fabric with chalk.

3. Cut outside your chalk lines, allowing a standard 1″ of fabric for your seam.

4. Lay the *cushion bottom* piece right side down on a flat surface and put the top piece over it.

5. Outline the top piece onto the bottom piece with chalk and cut out the bottom piece.

6. Mark your seam line 1″ inside the edges of the bottom piece with chalk.

Measuring and Cutting Boxing

Boxing is the sides, or thickness, of the cushion, and while it can be any height you wish, it is usually between 2½″ and 3″ on a puffy pillow and between 3½″ and 4″ on foam-filled or inner-spring cushions. Don't forget to add a seam allowance along all of the edges around the boxing. When you cut the boxing, be sure that the fabric is going in the same direction as the cover fabric on the front of the seat; obviously, the length of the boxing will equal the perimeter of the cushion plus a seam allowance at each end.

Joining the Pieces

1. Sew welting (see pages 147–148) to the seam line around the top and bottom cover pieces.

2. If you are filling the cushion by hand, start by pinning the boxing to the top cover at the center of its front edge, then work your way out to the front corners, around the sides and then the back edge, where the boxing should meet itself. Be very careful to keep the cover and the boxing equally stretched and smooth or you will get wrinkles when you stuff the cushion.

3. Machine sew the boxing to the top cover and close the boxing ends with a blind-stitched seam.

4. Locate the exact position of the corners on the top cover and mark a vertical line down the boxing strip to the bottom edge.

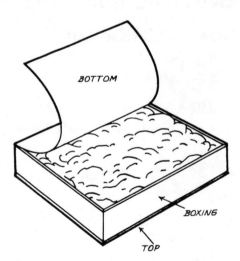

Sew only the front edge of the bottom cover to the boxing before you stuff the pillow.

5. Line up the corner of the bottom cover with the corner lines marked on the boxing, and pin the bottom cover to the boxing. Be sure to keep the cover and boxing equally stretched and smoothed.

6. Sew the front of the bottom cover to the front edge of the boxing, but leave the sides and back open.

Muslin Cases

Depending on the kind of cover fabric you are using and the material to be used in stuffing the cushion, it is sometimes advantageous to make a muslin case that fits inside the cushion. If you decide to make a muslin covering, it is made in the same way as the cover, except you do not have to use welting because the stitches will be hidden.

STUFFINGS

Springs

You can put practically anything inside a fitted cushion, including *pocket*, or Marshall, springs. Pocket springs are small coil-type springs that come encased in muslin or burlap pockets which have been stitched together. You can buy them at upholstery supply outlets and can use them in mattresses, cushions or even as the springs on chair backs as an alternative to tying down separate springs. Pocket springs are sold in all sorts of groupings and a variety of dimensions but generally the sizes used in cushions are 3″ in diameter and 3½″ in height. If you want to use them on a chair back, buy springs that are 6″ high. The dimensions of the spring set you use should be

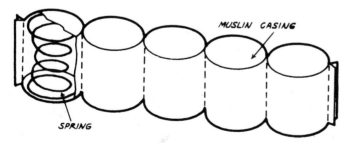

Pocket springs can be cut apart to fit in any size pillow.

between 1″ and 3″ shorter, both side to side and back to back, than the cushion cover, to allow for a layer of felted cotton between the boxing and the springs. Here's how to stuff your cushions with springs:

1. Place the cushion cover top-down on a flat surface.

2. Lay two or three layers of felted cotton on the top cover, leaving enough cotton to extend up the sides of the boxing. You can either use one piece of cotton that will fold up against the boxing, or cut separate strips for the sides.

3. Prepare a crowned layer of high-quality hair (see page 133) 2″ or 3″ thick and lay it on top of the cotton. You can, by the way, use medium- or soft-density foam instead of hair, provided you separate the springs and the foam with a thin rubberized pad.

4. Put the pocket springs on top of the hair and arrange the springs so they are evenly spaced side to side, but keep about 1″ of spacing between the springs and the front edge of the cushion cover.

5. Fill the spacing between the springs and the back edge boxing with strips of felted cotton.

6. Fill the spaces between the springs and the sides with as many layers of felted cotton as you need to produce firm side edges. Be careful not to pack the edges so hard that they prevent the springs from functioning properly. If the cushion has a half or full T at its front edges (to fit around the front of the chair arms), these are firmly stuffed with cotton and have no springs in them.

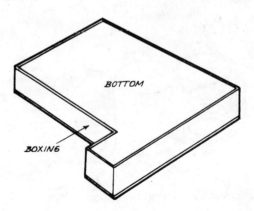

The T extensions of a cushion do not have springs, but are firmly stuffed.

7. The space between the front edge and the springs should be padded with enough felted cotton strips so that spring marks cannot show through the front boxing, but not so much that the springs are in any way inhibited.

8. Insert the same thickness of hair on top of the springs as you placed underneath them; then cover the hair with layers of felted cotton.

9. Pull the boxing up to meet the bottom cover and pin it to the cover at your corner marks. Again, be careful to keep all of the fabric smooth and equally taut. Also smooth or fill out any lumps or voids in the stuffing.

10. Pin the boxing to the bottom cover, always making certain there are no imperfections in the contours of the fabric. You can use a regulator to adjust the stuffing as you pin both sides and the back edge.

11. Tie two of the corners of the cushion tautly to a flat surface, so that the seam between them is stretched into a straight line, or purchase a commercial cushion stretcher to do the job. However you stretch the seam, you will now have to adjust your pins until the seam is straight and smooth. Then blind-stitch the boxing to the welt on the bottom cover. Do *not* sew either corner.

12. Stretch the opposite side seam and adjust the pins, then blind-stitch the welt to the bottom cover. Leave the corner and back seam unsewn.

13. Keep the cushion on a flat surface and work the stuffing toward the front edge. With most fabrics you can do this by slapping it and pushing the palm of your hand forward before you lift it from the cushion. Slap-push all of the

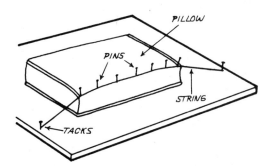

A seam can be stretched taut using heavy pins, tacks and string.

surfaces of the cushion until you have compressed the stuffing enough to show up any lumps or voids.

14. Remove whichever pins you need to in the back seam and use your regulator to break up any lumps you have discovered or to fill voids. Take a very close look at the front edge, the T extensions and the back edge, to be sure you do not have any "weak" corners or wrinkles.

15. Align the back cover and boxing and pin the seam. Stretch the seam and smooth out all wrinkles, then blind-stitch the back boxing to the bottom cover and the corners.

Feathers and Down

If you are stuffing your fitted cushions with down and feathers, you have to make a ticking case so that the stuffing cannot poke through the cover material. The ticking case is assembled in the same manner as the cover, but it should be slightly larger to guarantee fullness. Add 1″ to the length and 1″ to the width of the pillow if it is 12″ square or less. Add 5⁄16″ to both dimensions for every 6″ over the 12″-square size. For any cushion that is less than 12″ square, you can use a single ticking case, but larger units are usually divided into at least three compartments. Each ticking case becomes an 8″ wide tube that is placed in the cushion so that it runs perpendicular to the sides of the furniture. If you put the tubes in the cushion the other way, it is easier for the down to work its way toward the back of the seat cushion or toward the bottom of a back cushion.

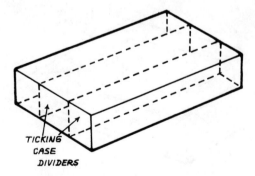

Ticking case tubes must be inserted from side to side so that the stuffing does not work its way to the front or back of the cushion.

TICKING
CASE
DIVIDERS

Making a Ticking Case

1. The ticking case should be made of downproof ticking. Each piece is cut according to the size of the cover pieces, plus the fullness allowance added to each of their dimensions. The boxing is the same dimensions as the cover boxing.

2. Sew the pieces together without welting, as the stitches will never be seen.

3. If you are using more than one ticking case in a cushion, there must be dividers between the tubes. The dividers can be a straight-edged strip of ticking that is as high as the cover boxing. But many upholsterers prefer to curve the top and bottom edges of the divider so that about 6″ from each end the strip becomes twice the height of the boxing.

4. Stitch the casing boxing all the way around the bottom piece.

5. Sew the dividers to the top piece.

6. Sew the top piece to the boxing along three sides, but leave the fourth side open until you have stuffed the case.

7. Stuff the compartments with down and feathers until they are all the same firmness.

8. Pin the unsewn seam and slap-push the casing until you have distributed the stuffing evenly.

9. Sit on the cushion. It should not feel lumpy or be too hard. When you get up, the cushion should rise back to its shape and show no signs of having been used.

10. Sew the pinned seam.

11. Push the ticking case into the cover, smooth the cover material and sew it.

Foam

You make a cushion with rubber and polyurethane foam the same way you make one with springs. The boxing can be anywhere from 2″ to 8″ high and you have the option of crowning (see page 133) one or both sides, or not crowning at all. If you decide to crown the cushion, there are three ways to do it.

Crowning with Concentric Layers

1. Measure and cut two pieces of foam for the top and bottom of the cushion, making them 1″ shorter than the cover along each edge.

2. Cut out the bottom inner piece, making it 4″ shorter in both directions than the bottom slab of foam.

3. Cut the top inner piece so that it is 4″ shorter in width and length than the bottom inner piece.

4. Center the two inner cores on the top slab so that you have a pyramid with 2″ wide steps along each side of the cushion.

5. Cement the inner cores to each other, and to the top slab.

6. Center the bottom slab over the smallest (top) inner core and cement it in place.

7. Cut out border strips that are 1″ thick and of the same dimensions as the cover boxing.

8. Apply cement to the backside of the border strips and to the edges of the top and bottom slabs. Wait until the cement becomes tacky.

9. Squeeze the edges of the top and bottom slabs together, allowing them to just touch, then center the border strips over the joint. You will have a

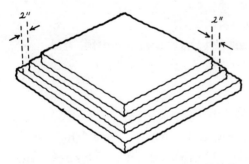

Each foam slab in a pyramid construction should be 2″ smaller on each side than the slab beneath it.

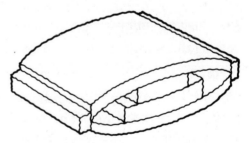

Glue boxing slabs to the joined ends of the top and bottom slabs.

border that is anywhere between ½″ and 1½″ narrower than the combined thickness of the slab edges. Be sure that the border is centered between the edges and that the strips do not overlap at the corners, then bond them to the edges of the slabs.

10. When the glue holding the edges together has dried, apply cement to the faces of the slab edges and the top and bottom edges of the border strips.

11. Allow the cement to become tacky and then squeeze the edges of the border strip and the edges of the slabs together, to form rounded corners all the way around the top and bottom edges of the cushion. Give the cement a minimum of four hours to harden.

12. When the cement has dried, and any areas softened by the cement will not tear, you can stuff the cushion in a muslin case or directly into the cushion cover.

Crowning with a Single Slab

1. Use a slab of foam that is equal to the thickness of the crown. Stand the slab on its side and draw lines that are half the height of the cover boxing inside the top and bottom edges. Thus, if your slab is 6″ thick and the boxing measures 4″, you will have one line that is 2″ inside the bottom edge and another line positioned 2″ inside the top edge. And there will be a 2″ space between the two lines. Draw your lines all the way around the slab.

2. Using a serrated bread knife or electric meat carver, slice a wedge out of the edges of the slab, using your lines as cutting guides. You can make the wedge as deep as you wish as long as you do not slice all the way through the slab, but the deeper it is, the shallower will be the slope of the crown. If you cut a very shallow wedge, you will have an abrupt crown edge. As you are cutting the wedge, be very careful not to compress the foam any more than is necessary, or you will destroy the cut.

3. Apply cement to both sides of the wedges and allow it to become tacky, then stick the sides together.

4. You will have pointed corners around the edges of the slab. These will be somewhat compressed when you stuff the slab in its cover, but if they really bother you they can be sliced off. The flat edge can then be covered with a 1″-thick strip of soft-density foam cut to the dimensions of the cover boxing.

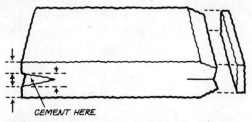

CEMENT HERE.

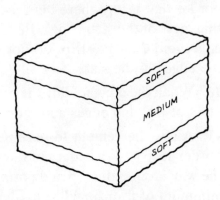

(Above) When making a crown from a single slab of foam, cement the inner surfaces of the wedge together. The points of the pieces can be cut flat and then faced with an edge slab that is the same height as the cover boxing.

(Right) Medium-density foam can be surrounded with soft-density slabs which will compress to form a crown under the cover fabric. The soft-density foam can also be trimmed at its edges.

Crowning with Three Foam Slabs

1. Use two soft-density foam slabs as the outer layers around a slab of medium-density foam. The medium-density slab should be the same thickness as the height of the cover boxing. The soft-density slabs should each be one-half the height between the top of the boxing and the crown.

2. Cut the slabs to the same dimensions as the cushion cover.

3. Sandwich the medium-density slab between the two soft-density pieces and glue them together.

4. Stuff the slabs into the cushion cover after the glue has hardened. The soft-density foam pieces should compress enough to form the crown, but if they don't, you can shape them slightly with a serrated carving or bread knife.

Getting Foam into Its Cover

Any time you use foam inside a pile fabric (such as velvet) you must encase the foam in muslin, or it will pull the pile fibers through its backing. Actually, a muslin case is helpful no matter what cover material is used, since it helps make the foam slide easily into the material. The case should be made the same size as the cover.

If you are not using a muslin case, you still ought to insert a layer of cotton or polyester fiber between the top of the foam and the top of the cushion cover so that the cushion feels less rubbery. You can also sprinkle talcum powder on all touching surfaces to reduce friction between the foam and the fabric it touches.

If you are making flat cushions and want them to have a slight crown, you can place a layer of cotton padding on either or both the top and bottom of the foam, making each layer slightly smaller than the one beneath it, then wrap a final layer of cotton or polyester around the whole cushion.

Throw Pillows

Boxed-edge throw pillows are made exactly like fitted cushions and can be stuffed with any material you wish, although springs are not usually used.

Single-welt pillows that are either rounded or have a knife edge will pull at their corners, because the center of the pillow is normally thicker than the edges. If you want to maintain right-angle corners on a single-welt cushion, you have to go through some extra machinations:

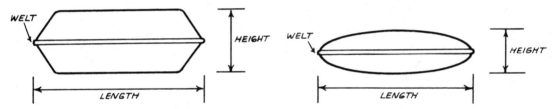

If a single-welt pillow is to have rounded corners the cover fabric will measure the length × the height of the pillow. The cover fabric for a knife-edge pillow measures the length of the pillow × ½ the height.

Making Right-Angle Corners in Single-Welt Cushions

1. Measure, cut, sew and then stuff the cushion.
2. Pin the corners so they are straight right angles.
3. Remove the stuffing.
4. Resew the cover along the lines you have pinned it.
5. Stuff the cushion again.

If you follow this procedure to make a muslin casing, you can then use the muslin as the pattern for your cover fabric.

(Right) Any box or hassock can be padded and used as a floor pillow.

(Below) After sewing the backrest together, leave it's back open to facilitate stuffing.

(Below right) A backrest can be constructed from foam or rubberized fiber and then covered with padding and a cover.

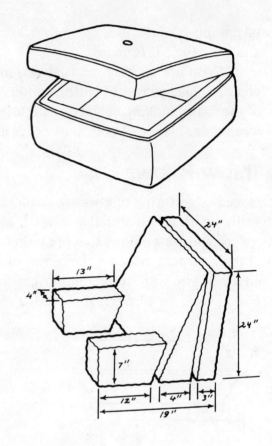

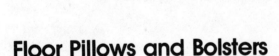

STUFFING

Floor Pillows and Bolsters

You can construct a floor cushion around any frame, such as a hassock or box, or in the same manner as you make fitted pillows. The frame should be covered with a layer of coarse fiber that gives the basic shape of the padding. Cover the fiber with as many layers of second and/or top stuffing as you wish and then fit covers around the stuffing and tack it to the frame.

Bolsters can be made in the same way as large floor pillows, but are kept as light as possible, because they are used on furniture and usually moved around quite a bit. There are two methods to make a shaped bolster such as an armed backrest:

Sewn-to-Shape Bolsters

1. Cut and sew the cover in the shape you want the bolster to be, but leave either the back or the bottom open.

2. Insert several layers of cotton or polyester padding against the insides of the cover.

3. Stuff the center of the bolster with coarse fiber or felted cotton, packing the space as firmly as possible.

4. Cover the back (or bottom) with a layer of cotton padding and sew the panel shut.

Cored Bolsters

1. Make a shaped core for the bolster by cementing together slabs of foam or any coarse, rubberized fiber. One of the best core materials is the foam found in insulating panels of picnic coolers and shipping cases.

2. Cover your core with layers of soft foam, cotton, or polyester.

3. Measure and cut the cover fabric pieces.

4. Assemble and sew the cover and put it over the core frame.

INDEX